JULIANA JONES

Meg & I; A Love Story
How Rescuing A German Shepherd
Healed My Broken Heart

First edition

ISBN (paperback): 979-8-9934690-2-7
ISBN (hardcover): 979-8-9934690-1-0

This book was professionally typeset on Reedsy.
Find out more at reedsy.com

Dedicated to all those who have rescued animals...
You're rock stars.

And to Marc, aka Noel, who broke my heart in a thousand million
pieces.

Same with my sister.

And my mother.

I forgive you.

* * *

And to my Father and Aunt Jo, thank you.

Preface

"I looked at all the caged animals in the shelter...
The cast-offs of human society.
I saw in their eyes love and hope, fear and dread,
sadness and betrayal.
And I was angry. "God," I said, "this is terrible!
Why don't you do something?"
God was silent for a moment
And then He spoke softly.
"I have done something," He replied.
"I created You."
-Jim Willis

I never realized the depth of my loneliness.

Until I got a dog.

I never understood how someone could love something so much, that they would go to the end of the earth to see its happiness.

Love, to me, was how it was in the movies. *That long lost kiss...*

The kiss in Footloose when Ren gets the nerve to kiss Ariel. Or that illicit kiss when Father Ralph de Bricassart succumbs to Meggie in the forbidden romance, The Thorn Birds. Or in WITNESS, when John Book and Rachel run to each other in the field and kiss. One kiss.

A kiss to last a lifetime.

Love to me was always feeling; a state of being...

I never realized it wasn't anything of the sort.

Real love was life in the hard places: getting up at 2 am when your dog needs to go to the bathroom. Trying to pick up his runs when he has diarrhea with a plastic bag, picking up her large loads; three, sometimes four, five times a day. Running into the woods after her when her favorite blue ball gets stuck in a thorn bush.

Her eyes looking up at me like, *C'mon, Mom, you can do it. You're only going to get pricked a thousand times!*

Love is realizing that when she gets scared, like when she hears thunder or a loud noise that sounds like gunshots and she goes cowering into her cage, that it's okay. That I actually love getting on my hands and knees and petting her; comforting her during these times, telling her in a soft voice that it's going to be okay.

Never having been married, I always lived life for myself. I was a gypsy; flying around from destination to destination, going on yachts, overseas, traveling the world, man after man, party after party, living for the moment. Never tie down, never lock down...

Never. Be.

Trapped.

I had three goals: no husband, no employer, no landlord.

And after I achieved two out of three, I got her: Meg.

She came into my life during a very hard period. I was too young to retire but I felt old… having lived a full life; a life only for myself. But now there was her, my big, beautiful German Shepherd beast.

She was fierce, loving, smart, strong, brave. And I never realized she would change my life in ways unimaginable.

Here is our journey.

And if you're reading this, and you have the time or the money to rescue an animal, please do it.

This book is written for you.

You will learn so much about yourself and about life; and through their eyes, see it so much differently.

* * *

One

Chapter 1

❧☙

"I'm getting a dog!" I tell my friend, Lorna.

"A dog?" she stammers into the phone. "They're a lot of work. Why?"

"I'm getting a German Shepherd! It's been a bucket list item and I'm doing it!" I'm so excited, nothing can deter my enthusiasm.

"A German Shepherd? Oh my God..."

I grin. "I know, it's going to be amazing. I'm picking her up tomorrow."

"What?! Tomorrow?! How did you find this dog? Are you even prepared?"

"I found her on the Internet. Prepared? What do you mean? I'm heading out to the store now to get her some treats."

"Treats?! You're going to need more than that! Did you research this, Juliana? She needs a cage, a collar, and are you potty training her? My God..."

1

Potty training her, I wonder. *What will that entail?*

"Lorna, I have it all figured out. I fell in love with her picture on the Internet and I've looked at thousands of dogs, and I'll call you once she's situated. Bye!"

I hang up. There was always a negativity to Lorna that I couldn't stand, but low and behold I decide to research a crate.

I didn't think of it and *what if the dog requires one?*

I decide to call my childhood neighborhood friend who use to have horses in her backyard. We've kept in touch all these years and I know she has a dog.

"Hey Katherine," I say, in a good mood, "It's Juliana, how are you? I'm getting a dog!" I blurt out.

She's happier for me than Lorna. "Oh my God, that's great! I'm so proud of you," she says. "You're not one for commitment or responsibility so this is a big step. Good for you!"

Not sure how to take that one. "Yeah, okay, hey, do you have a crate for your dog?"

"Yes, of course I do. Crates are very important."

"How do I get one? I'm getting a German Shepherd!" I say again, my voice rising from all the excitement.

"Wow. That's a big dog. That's a lot."

I hear concern in her voice. My heart drops a little. "Are you sure you can handle that?" I hear her ask.

"Umm, sure, yes! I've already made up my mind."

"Okay, how much does she weigh and how old is she?"

"I'm not sure, let me contact the rescue agency and I'll get back to you."

"Hey, what a minute!" she blasts. "Any updates on Hollywood making your movie?"

"Not yet," I reply, "but after nearly twenty years of slave work, I'm sure it's going to happen!"

Will it? I wonder.

"Great!" she replies.

"I"m here on the East coast only temporarily, to be boots on the ground for my parents since they're eighty! Eighty, can you believe it?! They need me!" I add.

But do they?

I text my mother: "Mom, I'm getting a dog!"

No response.

"Anyhow, Kat, better contact the agency," I say, "I'll call you later, bye," and I hang up.

I pull up the rescue agency's email on my phone and send another email. "Hi Ana," I write. She has almost the same name as I do, so I've been taking this as a good sign, "It's Juliana again. A couple of questions. When is the dog's birthday and how much does she weigh? I think I should get a crate."

She quickly writes back. "Yes, you definitely need a crate. You must put the crate in your car so the dog can ride home in it. And we're not sure of her weight or her birthday. The vet has her at approximately six months old."

Vague. Confusing.

I relay the information to Katherine who immediately texts me some links for crates to purchase online. One is a pink crate. It's adorable, I buy it right away, and have it shipped the same day.

When it arrives, the crate is too small and looks like something a cat would fit into.

I take a photograph of it, send it to Lorna, and out comes more negativity. "That German Shepherd will never fit in that cage! You need a big one! As in extra large! She's going to grow, you know? As in get huge! It's a GERMAN SHEPHERD!" she exclaims.

Darn.

I pack the pink thing up and send it back while ordering something quick at Walmart.

I am now living in South Carolina since I got blown out of my old apartment in St. Petersburg, Florida, where I was living for the past ten months, due to arguing with the landlord over a pest infestation and clamoring air conditioning unit.

I learned VERY FAST that the landlord/tenant rights were much different in the state of Florida than they were in California. I spent the last eighteen glorious years in Santa Monica in various rent controlled apartments pursuing my dream to be a screenwriter.

Even though I still paid rent, this guy forced me to move out and I lost my "sales job," during all this after they pressured me to make "Sales videos," starring yours truly, *me,* which I adamantly fought against, and surprise, surprise, even though you're #1 on the sales team selling cyber-security to hedge funds, I was FIRED.

It all happened so fast.

And all this was after I moved to Florida to win back the love of my life, Noel Sheffield, who was the star of my first novel/movie HEDGED; hence my eighteen year stint in LA, only for that to fall apart, and then Covid happened, and my life went off the rails.

Now I'm living in South Carolina; Mt. Pleasant, to be exact, in a small town where my sister lives off the Isle of Palms, where my father used to own waterfront property but has since sold, and moved back up north full time.

The South isn't for me, and I found Florida to be even worse.

My last job was delivering pizzas, but since I didn't like the cleaning of the kitchen (yes, that was part of the job), and

I couldn't fold the pizza boxes fast enough due to terrible arthritis in my fingers, I was fired.

It was a long fall from grace after rising to a Senior Vice President at a top Wall Street firm selling equities to hedge funds in my twenties and thirties.

Luckily, after a few good years on Wall Street, and having to file for disability, I learned that my monthly checks would be approximately $2598.

When I filed for disability, that seemed like a lot of money. But when you're living on it, it's an entirely different story.

Yet the checks would be ongoing, and they would afford food and vet bills for the dog, so nothing was stopping me now.

I wanted to do good for the world.

And given my predicament, I felt that rescuing a dog would be the best fit.

I end up finding a great cage. It's huge and I set it up myself which takes great strength and patience.

I also buy a bunch of dog toys, milk bones, and I set up couch cushions all over my floors so the dog doesn't always have to be in the cage. She can rest her tushy on my comfy cushies. LOL.

I'm so excited.

The next day, my first disability check hits my bank account, and I'm off to get my new dog!

Two

Chapter 2

꧁꧂

Meg was her name online. And when I saw her, I fell in love instantly.

I looked at thousands of pictures of different dogs all over the internet and she was the one I kept coming back to.

Even Ana, the rescuer, said to me over email, "It seems like Meg is the dog you like. So when you arrive, you can meet her if that's your choice."

I wanted to meet *all the dogs*; there was about six that needed homes at this rescue center in the middle of no where in South Carolina, but that's not how they worked. You pick one dog, and then they bring that dog out, and if it's a fit, you can take that dog home.

But don't forget the $450.00 CASH ONLY, they kept reminding me.

A part of me thinks this whole thing is a scam. That I'm

going to drive all the way out there; two hours, and get there and there will be no dog, they just take my money and abandon me.

Or worse.

Plus, the dog's name *is MEG*.

How strange.

If this isn't a scam, that's the first thing I'm going to change about her is *her name*. I will astutely name her "GEKKO," after Gordon Gekko from the movie WALL STREET.

Gekko, the German Shepherd.

As I drive out the next morning, I start to get nervous.

Will the dog like me? Is this a scam? Who are these people? What if they're crazy?

It's a long, windy drive on a highway where they're doing construction and everybody is driving too fast.

What if I can't find the place? What if I don't like the dog? What will it feel like if I drive all the way here and then all the way back with NO DOG?

Stay positive, I tell myself. A dog needs a home. *And you, with your disability checks, will take care of a dog.*

Plus, the doctors at the free medical clinic, since I had no job and therefore *no healthcare*, gave me a prescription for the dog. They said it would help me with any depression and help with my mobility issues. They were very PRO DOG.

I decide to listen to the radio, and the song by Natalie Merchant, "These are the days," comes on.

I'm instantly reminded of a video my mother used to play over and over again of her and my sister dancing on the beach to this music… My mother and my sister, swinging their arms and hugging each other, laughing and dancing by the wild ocean waves to this music.

They looked so happy and carefree...

There was never a video of me like this with my mother.

I turn the station.

I really hated that song.

After two long hours of driving, I finally I merge off the highway and I'm in the middle of no where.

This is the perfect set up, I think. These people really got me good.

I am in the woodsiest of woods and I am all alone because my useless sister wouldn't come with me after ignoring me for the entire year that I lived in her town.

We were always close up until she married some two bit banker from New Jersey who I couldn't stand from jump street. He was the wedge that came between my sister and I and things with us have never been the same since.

It bothered me a lot, just like leaving LA for Florida to see Noel bothered me after he read my novel, loved it, knowing he was the star of it, and then never even met up with me for a cup of coffee.

I wanted to see him after all this time. But he would not give me that.

So between the lost affair with him, and the broken relationship with my sister, my heart was in pieces.

But I was too busy getting fired from job after job, and then going to medical appointments to get the disability claim going, so I could survive. And that was a hell ordeal, one I wouldn't wish on my worst enemy.

Even I, with a Masters Degree from the University of San Francisco, California in Health Services Administration, could hardly navigate our broken, fragmented, pathetic healthcare system. It was a nightmare.

8

Never again, is all I can say, and when I leave this earth, I hope it's a quick exit and not a long and painful one depending on "the system."

I try not to go further down into the quicksand of my depression, and as I get closer to my destination, I decide that if Meg is a real dog who needs a real home, I will be upbeat and together and happy when I first see her; not a run down, depressed mess like I feel like inside.

No, if she's real, she will know nothing of my past.

Not of my failure as a screenwriter in Los Angeles after eighteen years of trudging there, nor will she know of all the money I blew in the stock market from a slight gambling problem, nor will she know of my broken heart over Noel Sheffield, or how my books never made enough money to support me, or how my sister completely abandoned me in my time of need, and finally, how my mother, who is the biggest thorn in my side, still to this day, for reasons unbeknownst to me, won't even speak to me on the phone.

No, I'm going to rescue a dog today, and become the greatest mother in the world.

Three

Chapter 3

I slowly merge off the highway and head down a long, narrow road that leads straight into the woods.

The trees go far up into the air, and yet the sun still shines through. I take this as a good sign and keep driving.

Why doesn't the GPS ever get the arrival time correct?

This trip should have taken under two hours, but now it's almost three hours and this rescue place is no where in sight.

I grow more and more uneasy the further and further I drive out.

When I researched the address over the internet, all I saw was a trailer and a tiny house that had a fence in the shape of a large circle, and inside of it, were eight dogs.

It looked weird. Yet again, I'm in South Carolina. *So what doesn't look weird?* I'm not in Manhattan or LA anymore, I remind myself. Loathing the thought.

I keep driving.

Stay positive, I tell myself. *I'm going to meet this dog and love it.*

But then I am reminded of internet dating and all those men I met who I couldn't stand from the second I saw them. Not exactly "couldn't stand," but knew they were not "it."

I was a keen judge of character and never wrong. But being wrong about a man online was one thing. So you suffer through a dinner which I always made fun. I am after all, *me,* and I am exciting and fabulous, but what happens if *I don't like this poor dog?*

Here I am out in the middle of no where. These people probably *need my $450.00* as they are trying to survive out here in the WOODS, but what do I do about the poor dog if I don't want it?

Sorry Mr. Dog, this is not a fit.

I'm going to leave you out here to suffer in Holly Hill.

Yes, that's the name of the town I'm heading to. Holly Hill, South Carolina.

As I drive farther and farther out, thinking further and further what a mistake this is, I curse out my sister who didn't take the ride with me!

Suddenly, I pass a tiny house on the road and am relieved to see and hear some signs of life, but then it's nothing again, just more woods and long roads.

Was that it? I wonder. *Was that the house Meg is at?*

There is nothing else out here! That has to be it!

I turn the car around.

Why isn't the damn GPS directing me correctly? Even they are confused and bothered!

Turning the car around is difficult because the road is narrow, and if I drive even a few inches off of it, I'm going to end up in a ditch.

I will die out here alone. No one will ever find me.

At this point, I'm wondering if this would be better anyhow. The better road. The "high," road. Go out without a bang. Just disappear. *Poof, gone!*

Stop with the negative thoughts, I tell myself. *I'm rescuing a German Shepherd today and it's going to be great!*

As I drive closer and closer to the one lowly house that's in the middle of no where, I see a fence and to the right of it, that trailer I saw on the internet.

This is it!

I attempt to pull in but there's no driveway. It's just grass and to get to the house, I have to maneuver my car over a tiny bridge that goes over a stream of water.

A man comes rushing out.

Ana told me that she was "too disabled," to meet me, so she would be sending her "long time partner, Reeves," to handle the "transaction."

I stop before the bridge and get out and wave to him.

I try to gauge him from afar. When I see him, I am put at ease. He's a little overweight; just an average middle aged man wearing a T-shirt and shorts.

He doesn't say anything.

I ask him to direct me over the bridge so I don't drive off of it and into the stream.

He agrees and stands in front of my car, and waves me onto his property avoiding said tragedy.

I don't know where to park but I guess with all of this open land, anywhere is good.

I exit the car and put on a happy face. "Hi Reeves! I'm Juliana, thank you so much for meeting with me today!"

He smiles but doesn't say anything.

I'm looking around for Meg. *Meg, where are you?*
Meg?

Now I'm really starting to think this is strange.

"Yeah, I made it out here, no problems," I add. "Really pretty out here," I add.

He still doesn't speak and is just staring at me awkwardly. "Umm, I brought everything you asked for, and I have it all in my car."

He nods.

This is weird.

"Where is the dog?" I finally ask, and hold my breath.

He looks towards the fenced-in pen. My eyes follow his.

I see all the dogs, but I don't see Meg because those aren't German Shepherds.

I look back at him.

"She's out back."

I nod.

"I'll go get her. You can sit down here," he says, pointing to the lonely picnic table in the middle of the front yard.

"Sure!" I reply, relieved. "I'll grab her treats in my car."

He nods and walks off.

I go back to my car and my heart is racing. I take everything out that I brought for the dog; her new collar, a huge dog pillow for her to sit on, a towel, some toys and a cute orange doll that squeaks.

I set up everything at the picnic table and I wait.

The sun is beating down on me. I look around at the dilapidated place and can't believe I'm here.

I am literally in the middle of no where and anything can happen. But something in my heart tells me I'm in the right place.

Something in my heart tells me that I'm meant to do this.

I hear the door open, and as I look back towards the house, *there she is.*

Reeves opens the flimsy screen door, and Meg steps out.

I suck in my breath. She's wobbling on her long legs, looking all around.

She follows close behind Reeves and she looks confused... "Oh, my God," I utter, as tears form in my eyes

She walks towards me and I get up from the picnic table and bend down.

I open my arms, and the dog comes running toward me and falls into my arms. I kiss her and hug her, filled with warmth and joy. She is beautiful. She is perfect.

I am madly in love.

As I cradle Meg, I sense her relief. I lean back against the picnic table and stare into her eyes, and I start crying.

She is licking my face and Reeves stares at us, and I have no words. I keep hugging her and I cannot believe it.

I have done so many things in my life. So many stupid things that have never worked out.

But this, this couldn't have happened any better.

I look up at Reeves. "Thank you," is all I can manage. Meg keeps kissing my face, and I say, "This is my dream. I have always wanted a German Shepherd and now she is here. I'll take her."

"You want her?" he repeats in a surprised tone.

"Yes, I want her. I love her."

I squeeze Meg again, and in this moment, I vow to take care of her and love her forever.

I take out my phone and take a selfie. I turn the phone

around to see the picture of us, and I look so happy. The smile on my face that has long disappeared since Covid, is now back.

I complete the paperwork with Reeves, and he leaves me with a small bag of dog food and another bag that has their rescue logo name on it, and some coupons and pamphlets.

I pay Reeves the money and the deal is done.

"Don't forget to get her spayed," he adds, "that is a part of the deal you signed."

"Yes, of course. Thanks again, Reeves, this is the best day ever!" I say, and my heart filled with joy.

Reeves helps me get Meg into the car.

I couldn't fit her massive cage in the car, but Ana said it was okay if I just put her in the back seat.

I think after all our back and forth, she didn't want this deal to fall through, and quite frankly, neither did I.

Meg's in the car, I'm ecstatic, and I can't wait to drive off. "Bye Reeves," I say, waving to him, "Thanks again!"

And as I head back over the bridge, Meg and I are off to start our new life!

Four

Chapter 4

Meg is irate in the car.
       She's panicked and using her long legs as tennis rackets batting everything in her sight. She keeps hitting the back seat with her paws and circling around, then she jumps up in the front passenger seat, sniffing me.

"Stay, Meg, stay," I command. I wonder why she is so agitated.

She starts whimpering.

"We're going home," I tell her. Home to my over priced apartment in what will be a big city to you in comparison to this joint.

Meg let's out this high pitched squeal that I have never heard coming from any animal before in my life.

Oh, my God, what is wrong with her?

"It's okay, honey, we're going to have a great life! I promise you that. I'm going to take care of you and love you and ...."

BAMMM!

She hits the clutch that's between us with her paw, and the car goes flying into neutral while I'm going forty-five miles per hour.

"Whoa! Meg, stop!"

She doesn't, so I pull over and stop.

I can't stay here for long because it's a one lane road and a car or more likely, a pickup truck, can come barreling into us. "Sweetie, what is it?"

She keeps circling in the front seat and whacking the dashboard with her paws. *How am I going to keep this dog under control on the highway?*

She's panting and whimpering and not settling down. *Why couldn't my damn sister come and help me with this?!*

Even though the dog is only six months old, she is quite big and strong. She whacks the clutch again and looks up at me.

"Stop!" I order, "Please stop it!"

After a few minutes, she calms down, and I start driving again. We make our way onto the highway, and now Meg is looking out the window. She must be wondering who I am and where I'm taking her.

The highway construction is still going on and the road has been thinned out to two lanes, but even in the slow lane, I can't keep up with the speeding traffic.

I try not to panic and the dog starts acting up again.

I'm extremely nervous, so I do the only thing I know to do which is BREATH WORK, from my meditation class.

"Breathe in," I say slowly, taking a long breath, "One, two, three, four.... Breathe out... One, two, three, four...."

I do this in the calmest voice that I can muster, hoping it has the right affect on the dog. "Breathe INNNNN, BREATHE

OUTTTTT….. BREATHE IN….One, two, three, four… BREATHE OUT…"

I do the best I can imitating my meditation instructor, and it actually works for both me and the dog.

I keep the radio off and do this at least two hundred times before we get home.

By the time we pull into a parking spot two hours later, the dog is comfortable and calm. I thank my lucky stars that we arrived home in one piece.

I turn off the engine and walk over to the other side to let the dog out. I open the door, hold her leash, and say, "Come on."

She gingerly jumps down and then she looks up at me. "What now? Where are we?" she is asking me with her eyes.

"My darling, we are home. This is your new home."

I fumble with the key fob and take her through a side door to get to my third floor apartment.

When I open the heavy door, Meg stands there and she doesn't move. She doesn't know what to do, so I enter first, and she follows.

When we approach the staircase, she stops and looks up at me again.

I realize she has probably never seen a staircase before in her life, and I can't help but smile. "This is a staircase and we climb it, okay?"

She looks confused.

Clumsily, she puts one foot up onto a stair, and then the next. She's going slow, but by the sixth step, she gets the hang of it. Her tongue is hanging out and she looks happy.

We make it to the top of the stairs, I open the hallway door, and we finally arrive to my apartment.

At my front door, I unclip her leash, let her inside, and I'm excited to see her reaction.

The dog starts walking around, sniffing every corner. "Welcome home, honey!!"

I close the door to my bedroom so she can't go in there, and she's happy to roam around in the big living room and open kitchen as she looks all around.

I go her over to her cage, and explain, "This is yours, okay? This is your big cage."

She goes inside and sits down. She has a stupid, goofy grin on her face, and I am happy. All my hard work in planning this is paying off.

"Are you hungry?" I ask, "I got you some food."

I go into the kitchen and pull out the large bag of Purina puppy chow for large breeds that I was told to purchase in the chicken flavor.

I put two scoops in a bowl and put it down in her cage because with all the research I did, I learned that she is supposed to eat in her cage so she associates her cage as a safe and happy place that is her own.

She devours the food in seconds. She actually seems starving and she looks very thin. I can see her bones.

I start throwing her balls and I take out my phone and start taking photos and videos, and send them to my parents.

My mother responds with a bunch of happy emoji's, and Meg is running all around, and I did it!

I rescued an animal and gave her a new home!

Five

Chapter 5

I decide to take a nice, hot shower while keeping Meg in her cage and when I get out, I put on clean sweatpants and T-shirt, and let the dog out.

It has been quite a day already, and I'm ready to relax and watch the news.

I start to make a salad in the kitchen. I have a perfectly ripe avocado, and I as start to peel it, I notice it really is lovely. I love a perfect avocado!

I wash lettuce and blueberries, and then cut up some carrots. As I move back and forth from the refrigerator to the counter, I get this creeped out feeling that something is following me.

The cabinets are dark and so is the wood flooring, and so is the dog, and when I look down, it actually IS THE DOG following me.

She is mimicking my every move!

A few times, I almost trip over her!

20

Oh, my God! It's like she's watching and monitoring my every step. *Why is she following me like this?*

For someone who lives alone, who is ALWAYS ALONE and doesn't answer to anybody, this is quite a realization.

I decide to ignore it and when I sit down on my big couch and put my feet up to dig into my salad, Meg starts doing circles beside me.

I'm watching her trying to figure out what the hell she is doing and then all of the sudden, after about the seventh circle, SQUIRRRTTTTTTT, out comes loads of diarrhea. All over my rug!!! OH MY GOD!!!! STOP! STOP!

"HELP!!! HELP!!!!!!!!"

I don't know who I'm calling out to for help, and I am stunned and disgusted.

Once she starts letting it all out, there's just no stopping her.

There's no time to wrestle her up and get her down the three flights of stairs and out the heavy door to go.

The stench is horrific and I'm appalled. I throw up my salad on the counter and I need to clean this shit, *literally,* UP.

Luckily, I bought a garden shovel at Walmart with everything else I had purchased for her, and I scoop up the soup ladened crap and throw it down the toilet.

Then I get on my hands and knees with rags and paper towels to scrub it out. It's a thick, beige carpet and the diarrhea is deep in there, and there is no way it's going to come out.

My lease isn't up until May and it's only January, and I cringe at the thought of having to live with this until then.

After this explosion, I need another shower, and afterward, I try to focus on myself again.

I check my emails to see if there are any emails back from Hollywood.

Nothing.

I return to the kitchen to make some Chamomile tea and every time I turn around, I sense the shadow. I can't shake it and finally, I look down and there's the dog again!

I don't have her little tags that I ordered online which would cause some kind of "jingle sound," so she is like a silent, stealthy black panther stalking me. It's a surreal feeling.

Her deep brown eyes penetrate me, always asking, *"What are you doing, Mom?" "Why are you doing that, Mom?" "Couldn't you do it better, Mom?" "What's wrong with you, Mom?"*

I find myself confused in her presence. I try to call out her name out, "Gekko," but it doesn't stick. I can tell right away, she seems more like a "Meg," than anything due to her princess, goofy like ways.

Still, I think I will give this more time to play out, and hope she toughens up and turns into a "Gekko." We'll see.

It has been a long day, and tomorrow morning we hit the vet first thing, so she needs to turn in.

After a quick walk around the apartment complex, I learn that she's really good with walking on her leash. She naturally pulls me in a way which really eases the pressure on my lower back, helping my arthritis. The doctor's were right.

When we get back inside, I tell her, "It's bedtime," and I put a treat down in her cage and when she goes inside, I gingerly close the door. "Good night, my darling, sweet dreams."

Meg sits down and I hope she doesn't end up barking all night long. I do need my beauty sleep and I have heard horror stories of that happening.

I close my eyes and fall off to a deep, dark sleep, knowing my little love beast is just outside my door.

Six

Chapter 6

I wake up the next morning, excited to see "mah babe." I jump out of bed, open my bedroom door, and peak out at her cage.

Meg's sitting in the exact same position that I left her in last night.

Her large beige paws are set evenly in front of her, and her head is just staring straight ahead. Her eyes are wide open, and it doesn't appear as if she closed them all night.

"Good morning, my love! How was your first night sleep in your new bed?" I go to her and open her cage door.

She stands, wobbly on her feet, and looks around. It looks like she's asking me, "What happened? Where am I?"

"My darling, what a gorgeous day it is out there! Let's take you downstairs so you can do a wee wee."

I move to the front door where her leash is waiting. I grab it and go back to her and snap it on. "Okay, let's go."

She stares at me, not knowing what I'm talking about. I am worried she's going to start doing those "circles," again and take more dumps on the floor.

"Now, sweetheart. Let's go." I gently try to pull her on the leash.

She's not budging. "Come on, honey, I'm going to go outside and have fun, are you coming?"

The word "fun," seems to resonate with her.

She follows me out the door and instead of heading for the elevator, I make my way toward the staircase again.

Lord knows what she's capable of when being trapped in an elevator with other people, and I'm claustrophobic anyhow, so the stairs it is, and always will be from this moment on. But we don't make it there because she stops and hunches over.

Oh, no.

Too late.

She pees all over the hallway, with some getting onto a neighbor's doormat. "Oh, no! No! No! No! NOOOOOO!!"

The damage is done. There's a large puddle all over, and I take out some napkins from my jacket pocket and wipe it up.

I wonder if I should even bother taking her downstairs now, but she needs to learn that was a bad move.

"Sweetheart, bad. BAD! Let's go OUTSIDE so you can do your business THERE."

The sun is blaring when we exit outdoors, and being that it's South Carolina, it's already hot and muggy and nasty.

People are getting into their cars, driving to work, and I'm standing there in raggedy clothes holding onto this dog for dear life.

"Cute puppy," I hear someone say, which lights me up.

"Oh, thank you! I just got her," I add, and I look back down at Meg, trying to get her to go to the bathroom.

How do they know she's a puppy? She looks pretty huge to me, even though she's on the thin side.

We walk around the parking lot with no direction, like, "A complete unknown," lol, and I decide it's time for her food and take her back upstairs to eat.

She's getting used to the stairs already and climbs up with no problems, so I'm taking this as a good sign that she's a quick study.

"Time for your yum yum, my darling!" I say as I scoop out two large cups of dry kibble that looks bad and smells even worse. "Deeee-licious!" I coo.

She devours it in one second. *Literally.*

I'm wondering if I should give her more, but we have an early appointment at the vet and I don't want to be late.

Before she knows it, she is back in the front seat of my car, and she stares out the window. She's much calmer today than she was yesterday.

We arrive to the Vet in Mt. Pleasant, South Carolina and go inside. The bells on the door ring, announcing our arrival, and the crew comes out. "Oh, how cute! Look! Look a German Shepherd!" they all chime.

I grin, "Isn't she adorable?"

"Yes! Yes!" they all agree.

"Put her on the scale and let's get her weight," a chunky technician says.

I lead Meg onto the big scale and a large 38 number pops up on the digital screen.

"She's thirty-eight pounds!" another girl croons.

We're put into the medical room and wait for the doctor to come in. I brought Meg's large gray pillow and I sit down with her on the pillow so she's not afraid.

We wait and wait, and I pet her and give her love. "Don't be afraid, honey, this is nothing. You're going to be fine."

Meg just sits quietly. There is something that is very docile about the dog. She's very calm and quiet.

The doctor walks in, and I look up.

For whatever reason, I don't like her the second I see her. She's an uptight blonde who moves in a hurried, frustrated manner. She is followed by a team of four girls who treat her like she's God.

The staff huddles in the room with Meg and I, and I feel stifled and I wonder if the dog is getting the same bad vibe.

"Okay, so," the veterinarian begins. "I see you have a German Shepherd."

I nod, "Yes, I rescued her," I add, as if that should explain it all.

"I see," she snips, and then says, "These dogs can be a LOT OF TROUBLE, and they must be handled CORRECTLY from the GET GO."

I suck in my breath, and nod.

"What's her name?"

"Gekko," I muster, "but her name at the shelter was Meg," I add. I hand over the file of paperwork that they gave me.

"I think she has some shots, but she needs some other ones, it's all listed there on the papers," I say.

The doctor sifts through Meg's paperwork at high speed and practically throws the file at one of the young girls. "Add this into our system," she demands.

The girl walks out, seeming relieved to be out of her sight.

"What you're going to need to do IMMEDIATELY," she orders, "is socialize the dog. Take her to Home Depot and

Lowe's. There you can walk up and down the aisles with the dog. Make her know that people are okay."

But *they're not okay.*

I nod.

"What is she eating? She's very thin and malnourished."

"I have her on Purina Pro Plan, chicken. But she's scratching a lot and in the research I did, I read that German Shepherds can have an allergic reaction to chicken."

She doesn't seem to know anything about this and doesn't respond.

She bends down to the dog by my side and looks at her teeth. "Her gums are bleeding. This is a problem. She may have been abused."

Abused? I think, alarmed. *No, impossible.* The dog is fine.

This lady is a crackpot. "What shots does she need?" I ask, wanting to get out of here as quickly as possible.

One of her minions comes over and sticks a vaccine chart in my face. Some of the names are checked off.

With her pen, she points, "Gekko had this one and this one, but needs this one and this one."

I'm not sure what any of this means, but hope they know what they're doing. Although "hope," is never a strategy.

"Okay, let's get it done."

Meg is well behaved for the shots and we pay hundreds of dollars to blow out of there.

"Get her a feeding bowl," the doctor concludes, "so she slows down her eating and doesn't get digestion problems."

I nod. "Okay, bub-bye."

We get home and I'm drained. I sit on the twin bed that I have in my living room that's by the window.

The movers in Los Angeles couldn't move my beautiful

couch out the door; they said it was too big, and when I arrived in Florida, I bought a twin bed to use until my stuff arrived, and I never replaced the couch so I have been using this bed as my couch.

It's very comfortable, and Meg also finds it comfortable, and she is curled up by my feet.

I turn on CNBC stock market news and watch the market as the dog stares out the window.

Often she will turn to glance at me with a look of love.

I worry when the next shit will arrive and vow to time it perfectly next time.

I spent a good fifteen minutes cleaning up another mess she made in the hallway, and I can't be bogged down any further with cleaning up her urine and dog poops.

I turn back to the market. I'm short and losing money. I've been short for the past five years. I keep averaging down to no avail with any money I have, longing volatility, waiting for a crash. It has been a bad trade.

I turn back to the dog. I can't be short there.

I cannot afford to lose my patience.

Seven

Chapter 7

꧁꧂

I arise early the next morning not because I want to, but because the beast needs to go outside and relieve herself.

I am not sleeping well at all in this "luxury apartment," whereby I spend $2,000 a month on a one bedroom apartment because unbeknownst to me, my bedroom sits right above the main door to the building.

Within three months of signing the lease, management decided to "upgrade the key fob magnet," which meant the magnet to slam the door was magnified to ensure the door would securely close.

Unfortunately, it caused the loudest slamming noise known to man.

Management despises me because I have videotaped it and complained about it numerous times.

They repeatedly said, "There's nothing we can do about it, and YOU'RE the only one complaining." They also refused to move my unit.

ALSO, in the middle of the eight hundred unit complex, sits a MASSIVE trash compactor.

Desperate as I was to find housing, I brushed aside the fact that this could potentially pose a problem. *Big mistake.*

This trash compactor sits directly across from my unit, but because they have it concealed in a massive brick-like structure, you don't exactly realize it is *there.*

Also what I didn't realize, is that after I signed said lease, *of which there is no way you can get out of,* is that the trash compactor COMPACTS ALL THE GARBAGE FOR EIGHT HUNDRED UNITS every third time somebody throws their trash out.

This happens multiple, if not hundreds of times throughout the day and night. The rumbling of the machine sounds like an earthquake, shaking and rattling my apartment, and waking me up at of a sound sleep nightly.

It is an absolute nightmare.

Tenants that live here come and go during all hours of the night, discarding their trash, walking their dogs or simply going to or coming home from work, so between the key fob magnet door SLAMMING and the trash compactor COMPACTING, the place is LIVING HELL.

It is the worst, I mean THE WORST PLACE I have ever lived. And I have lived in some dumps.

On the upside, people have lots of dogs here, so I often walk around to observe their behavior and ask questions.

The next morning on my outing with Meg, I see a young man with black hair who's chubby and lazy looking. He has a black dog who looks just as lazy, and he is moving as slow as him. "Hi," I say awkwardly, as I approach.

His dog is bent into a shrub, taking a turd. "Is that your dog there?"

He nods, with a look.

"What a cutie pie!" I coo. "How old?"

"Five," he says in a monotone, annoyed tone.

"Oh, wow! Five years old. Great age! What kind of dog is that?" I need to ask lots of questions, mainly about size and stench of the turd, so I'm trying to establish rapport.

But it doesn't work out.

He turns, pretends he doesn't hear me, and moves on.

I turn and see somebody else who has one of those mini white fluff dogs walking around. When she sees me approaching with my big, black German Shepherd beast, the little poof ball starts barking. *Really? Do you think you have any shot here?*

Undeterred, I make my way over. "Hiiiiii…."

"Yes?! Yes?!" she keeps asking, petrified, as I get closer.

"Hi! How are you?!"

But before I can say anything, she and her tiny, white annoyance turn and walk in the other direction.

The next person I approach, I sneak up behind them so they cannot escape.

This girl has two big dogs. One looks like a Husky, the other is brown. "Hi!" I say, grinning, "I love your dogs!"

"Thanks!" she responds. "The big one is my boyfriend's, and this one is mine," she says pointing to the smaller brown dog.

"I see." I put my hands on my waist, as if I am doing some research. "What do you feed it?" I ask. "I have mine on the Purina Pro Plan chicken but she's been scratching."

"Ummm, this one is part German Shepherd, so we stay away from all things chicken."

"Yeah! That's what I read! That they can be allergic," I agree, and I'm glad she is so friendly.

She nods. "It's true. It's really not good for them at all, I found." She starts naming off brands that she likes of which I have never heard of, and as we're talking, one of her dogs bends over and dumps.

I watch as she scoops up the large turds. I notice she is using one bag to grab them, and then she turns it inside out around her hand and ties it up in one, swift maneuver.

I'm fascinated.

I am carrying around a garden shovel so I can put said turds into the shovel and then dump them into the plastic bag that are conveniently lying around in the Turd stations all around the complex.

I make a mental note to try it this way.

"Well, good luck with your dog!" she says, "Have a nice day!"

"You too!"

Meg and I head for the clubhouse because I need a latte and there's a free machine there that makes all kinds of sweet, delicious drinks with the push of a button. You just have to bring your own cup.

This is a hassle when I am trying to control the dog on her leash, hold her turds and my clean coffee cup at the same time.

When we get inside, there is no one in line for the coffee machine, and I place my cup under the spout and start pressing buttons. I am very focused and don't realize I let go of Meg's leash.

When I look down for her, I realize she is no longer beside me.

I look up and see her roaming the room, sniffing, and getting into everything. "Come back on the chain, please, honey," I say.

She realizes for an instant that she is free! She suddenly gets this crazed look on her face and when I move closer to her, she moves in the opposite direction of me.

"Meg, honey, that's not allowed. Please come back on the chain," I say, more seriously this time.

No luck.

And in an instant, she starts going crazy!

She begins running around the clubhouse doing spins and circles and jumping on all the furniture! I can't control her.

"Hey! Stop that! STOP IT !!!!

She picks up speed, hurling herself across the room, and as I watch, stunned, I look around to see if there are any video cameras. I can't tell.

"STOP! CONTROL YOURSELF!!!!

Meg won't stop. She is going mad. I cannot believe it. "Meg! Calm down! Get back here!"

But she's unstoppable. "What's gotten into YOU!?"

She's running all over the expensive couches, jumping up and down at a record clip, and then she flies into mid-air landing on her long legs. She races from one side of the room to the next, jumping on and off everything in her path until she is out of breath.

"What is. GOING. ON?!!!"

It's all happening so fast, it's as if someone gave this dog a large inhalation of cocaine and she is going bonkers. I don't know what to make of this behavior.

As I try to get control of her, her leg gets wrapped around an electrical cord of a very expensive lamp and the lamp goes flying and falls to the ground.

I hear the crash and close my eyes. *Oh, shit.* If she broke it, I do not have the money to pay for it.

I walk over to the lamp.

It's a miracle! It's still all in one piece! I pick it up and put it back on the table and manage to get a hold of the dog, returning to my hot latte and I take two large gulps. *Ahhh, the coffee is delicious.*

Relief is immediate.

I see someone entering the clubhouse and they didn't witness a thing. Luckily.

I wonder if what she just did was the "ZOOMIES," I read about.

"Oh, hiiiiiii," I say in my friendliest voice to this older woman entering, ignoring the fact that we almost just destroyed the place.

I whip out my treats, remembering what the veterinarian said about going to Lowe's and Home Depot. No need to go there when there is plenty of socializing to be done right here in the clubhouse.

The older woman with gray hair is carrying her cup and moving toward the coffee machine. Once she has her coffee, I ask "Do you mind?"

I extend my hand with the treat. "I would really appreciate it if you can give this treat to my dog."

She grins, and says, "Oh, I loves dogs!" and fusses all over Meg. She hands my dog the treat, and Meg loves it. "Good girl," I praise.

I smile. I have this all under control.

I hand the woman more treats and she does this over and over for me again. I thank her and when we make our way back outside, Meg still hasn't dumped yet and I'm wondering why.

She urinated on the floor before we made it out of the

apartment this morning *again*, so that's not happening out here either.

I'm already exhausted and don't think it's even 7:30 a.m.

We go back upstairs and I make my way into the shower.

I leave Meg in the cage so she can't do further damage, and while I'm in the kitchen making a pot of strong coffee, there she goes, diarrhea again all over my floor.

Eight

Chapter 8

"I can't stand it!" I tell Lorna. "How long does this potty training take!? I am not sure I am cut out for this! She is not learning ANYTHING and she is just making messes. Yesterday, she chewed the cord to my salt lamp! My salt lamp, Lorna! I lugged that with me all the way from LA!"

"Oh, just buy another one," she chirps. "This is what happens when you get a dog. They're a lot of work. I told you!"

"Yeah, yeah…" I can't take anymore of her 'I told her so's,' so I hang up and call my friend Rick out in LA.

"Ricko!" I say, overly excited, sounding unlike my usual self. "I miss you! How are you? How is LA?"

"It's shit," he says in his monotone voice. "It's all shit."

"Really? Still?!"

"That's right. You did good by leaving."

"I know it! The place was a DISASTER WHEN I LEFT! Just a DISASTER! I LOVE THE EAST COAST!! LOVE IT!!!!"

36

"What's up with you. Talk to me, I can tell something's wrong."

He's absolutely right. You know those people who sound overly happy that you can't stand? Those ones who claim "LIFE IS GREAT!" "REALLLLLY GREAT!!!" When you know, underneath there are some serious undercurrents. Well, that's me, right now, and I'm grateful I have my buddy Rick to call me out on it.

"Yeah, I got a dog," I admit.

"You what?!"

"I got a German Shepherd."

"A German Shepherd!? Geesus. Get rid of it!"

"What?!"

"Give the dog to a friend, and get back here to LA pronto," he says.

"Give the dog TO A FRIEND?! What friend?! Who?! I just rescued this dog!"

"What gave you an idea to do THAT?!" he blasts.

I glance out the window and then back at Meg who's lying on the floor looking at me.

"I don't know," I reply, softly. "She is adorable though, but you're right, this was a big mistake."

I feel guilty after saying that and to cover up my mal feelings towards said dog, I play ball with her for the next two hours while I gaze at CNBC.

I await a massive stock market crash so I can make some money on these derivatives that I'm holding, and somehow, get out of this predicament.

Nine

Chapter 9

T he next morning, despite being woken up about fifteen times due to the trash compactor compacting and the front door slamming, I'm in a better mood. I'll forget Rick and his clandestine plans of giving the dog away.

What kind of person does that anyway?

I decided what I needed was a schedule. An ironclad schedule for me and the dog.

I get up early so Meg would not even THINK about the fact that she needs to relieve herself.

I open her cage door and sing her praises and hurry and attach her leash, and we begin our decent down the hallway to the staircase.

Then, she starts the "circling."

In the hallway. Oh God, NO! NOT HERE! NO!!!! WAIT UNTIL WE GET OUTSIDE!!!

Too late, she keels over, lifting her hind legs and diarrhea comes spewing out all over another neighbor's doormat.

Omigod!!!!!!! I am mortified. I cannot believe it. The stench is unbearable. It is watery and oily and I have no idea how I'm going to clean this up.

I run back into my apartment and put the dog in the cage and grab my garden shovel with a paper shopping bag, cleaning fluid, and a roll of paper towels.

I run out to the neighbor's door, PRAYING they do not see this or have a "Door cam," on their peep hole. I get on my hands and knees and start lifting the turd into the paper bag with the shovel and scrub out the rest. However, there's NO POINT. It's ruined and I can't remove the brown spot that won't come out of their doormat.

I keep at it and do the best I can. In fact, I clean it so well, there is only a hint of catastrophe left.

I run back inside to get the dog, while leaving the crapped bag in the staircase, realizing she still needs to urinate.

I take with me a handful of treats, and when we get back downstairs, she urinates in a spot by the tree. "Good girl!" I coo. "Very nice," although I am still reeling from the mess she made moments earlier.

I am no mood for a latte, and in my jacket pocket, I keep a rubber ball, so we make our way over to the park.

There are many of them around our apartment complex, but the biggest one is on the far side of the lake where there are large alligators, and we make our way over there.

There is a lone chair there, and I sit in it as the sun comes up and throw the ball to the dog. I notice how fast she can run, and she's like lightning. When I throw the ball in the air, she can jump about ten feet high and catch it. It's impressive.

"Nice!" I say, "Gekko," trying to use her name but as I watch her, she hardly looks like a Gordon Gekko at all.

She's too pretty. Too docile. Too proper. In her own weird way, she's sort of a goof ball.

She comes back over to me, her tongue hanging out, and she stares at me. When I try to reach for her ball, she covers it with her large paws

I laugh, and try again.

She covers it and I can't get it. I laugh harder, realizing how strong and quick she is. "Don't you want me to throw the ball?" I ask.

She tilts her head, and then she gives in, and I throw it as far as I can.

Meg dodges off after it, and I look up into the sun and let it hit my face. This isn't so bad, I think. It will get better, I tell myself. *Won't it?*

On our way home, I see a guy standing by a tree while his dog is taking a shit. The dog is about Meg's size and I'm desperate for some answers so I make my way over. "Ohhh, hiiiiii!" I stammer. "How are you?"

I look over to him, but more importantly, I am trying to get a view of his dog's stools, wondering *why are Meg's yellow and orangey color? Why aren't hers formed?*

As he bends down to pick them up, I say, "Wait a minute!"

It startles him.

"Can I take a look at those?"

"Look at…. *what?*"

I'm standing there in a baseball cap, and Meg and I are wearing white matching bandanas around our neck.

"At your dog's…." I'm not sure what word to use: Shits? Turds? Craps? Logs? Dootz? "Bowel movements…?" I ask.

He looks at me as if I'm nuts.

"You see," I continue, "it's just, my dog, she really hasn't had a formed turd since I got her two weeks ago."

"It's probably her food."

"Her food?" I ponder.

"Yeah, switch it up. What do you have her on?"

"Purina pro plan chicken," I tell him.

"Try something else. We use Blue Buffalo and it works great."

"Great! I'll do that! Thanks so much!" and as I bend over to check out the turds, they are beautiful. A rich brown color and formed well into three large log size dumps.

We take off and I go back to my apartment so I can get my wallet and we make our way over to Walmart.

It's only a few blocks away if I cut through the hotel parking lot.

I come up with a quick plan, that I if I can return the Purina Pro crap, I will need something to lug it with since the bag weighs about ninety pounds. So if I buy a new wagon at Walmart, I can come back, grab her old food, put it in the wagon, return it, and buy the new food, and lug it all home in the wagon, all while taking the dog with me.

The first run goes well.

I find a nice wagon to purchase, but when I return with the rotten food, the parking lot is filled with next level undesirables. They are all eying me with the dog as I walk past, wheeling my wagon.

Then I realize, hey wait a minute. I've got a German Shepherd on my arm! A killer German Shepherd security dog, so watch it!

I stand up straighter and prouder, as me and the dog make

41

our way through the Walmart parking lot.

Returning the food is an ordeal; the "customer service," still isn't open yet, there's already a long line, and I still have to buy the new food. I decide to use the extra time to buy garbage bags so I can cover my floors with them.

When I get to the dog food aisle, they don't even have the brand that the guy recommended so I take a stab and try something else.

When we leave Walmart, I realize that if I'm ever debating killing myself, all I need to do is to go into Walmart and spend five minutes inside.

That will secure said decision. I hated the place. Between those fluorescent lights, the people, the long aisles, the millions of products from "overseas," never being able to find what I need, and those employees with those nasty BLUE VESTS, it just roiled me. The whole experience. Never have I even lived in a town before Florida that had a Walmart. San Francisco eight years, Manhattan eight years, LA eighteen years. *How did I get here? What wrong decisions got me here?*

The dog is in a hurry to get back home and she is leading the charge, pulling me, as I'm trying to balance the cart with all her food and garbage bags in it.

As we cut up again through the hotel parking lot, and back down the side road, Meg seems to know exactly where our apartment is.

When we get inside, I unload everything, cover up my entire floors with trash bags, and I feed her.

She gobbles up the food in an instant, and instead of taking a shower, I decide to use my Shiatsu machine which plugs into the wall.

I sit on the floor with it and let it run over my sore arthritic back. As I'm doing this, Meg thinks it's a great opportunity to play ball, so as I have one eye on CNBC, and one eye on my phone looking at my cratering derivatives that I'm holding on volatility, I keep throwing her rubber ball in the air and she brings it back.

She chews the ball, and waits for me to throw it again. But as I'm looking down at my phone, I hear ZZZSZZZZZZ, ZZZZZZZ and I look up. Sparks start flying!

I also smell smoke! I look down at Meg, and in that one minute that I wasn't looking at her, she had chewed the electrical cord of my Shiatsu machine! I cannot believe it and I'm hoping she didn't swallow any! This all happened in three seconds!!!!!

The machine is destroyed and there is no fixing it. It is shocking we both didn't get electrocuted or blown up!

I put her back in her cage and take a shower, frazzled and at my breaking point.

When I get out, I remove the beast from the cage and sit back down on my couch by the window.

I tell myself, "I can start my day over at anytime," and I psychically remove all the bad vibes from hours before.

I watch TV and play on my iPad. And just as I think I'm in the clear and we had a semi-good day, I look up, and the dog is DOING THE CIRCLES AGAIN! OH NO! NO MEG NO!!!!!!

She clicks up the trash bag with her nails, keels over on her hind legs, and goes in the exact spot she has gone in since she arrived.

FLLLLLLLLLLLL GHGHHGH CRAP ALL OVER MIXED WITH DIARRHEA ALL OVER MY FLOOR! MISSING THE TRASH BAGS.

Ten

Chapter 10

I come to the conclusion that the dog is not happy here. That she was much better out in Holly Hill where she had grass and greenery and plenty of room to run and play next to her trailer and she was with all of her brothers and sisters.

I decide to Google, "How many people return their dog after getting it?" and I'm surprised to read the high amount. 7% to 20% of adopted dogs are returned to shelters. This means that between one in five and one in fourteen dogs end up back in the shelter after being adopted.

Wow. *So I'm not the only one suffering.*

I read on and learn that the number of animal adoptions is also in a decline, and this decline is a contributing factor to the number of animals euthanized in shelters.

However, 80% of people who adopt a pet from a shelter, consider it to be the most rewarding thing they have ever done. And some surveys indicate that over ninety million households have a least one pet.

Hmmm.

Interesting. If they can do it, I can, I think.

Can't I?

No, I can't.

I need an iron clad plan. Ricko was right. Said dog is a nuisance and I just can't handle it.

I'm trapped, she's a lot of work, she doesn't like apartment living and that's the best I can offer her, and finally, I don't know what the HELL I'M DOING.

I need to do something with the dog but pawning her off on a "friend," is not an option when you have no "friends."

I come up with something else. A grand plan. One I will enact and it will work brilliantly.

I pick up the phone and call the police.

"Mt. Pleasant Police Department," I hear a young man say.

"Hiiiiii!" I say, "This is Juliana Jones calling! How are you today?!"

"Thank you, ma'am for asking, I'm just doing fine. How can I help you?"

This is my good service, I tell myself. I am such a good citizen and pro-funding the police with a great dog. A great Houdini German Shepherd.

"Oh, WOW! I have fantastic news. Just fantastic!!! I can't even believe how excited I am to relay this fantastic news! Who's in charge over there?"

"Ummm, what's this news? How can I help?"

"Well, you see," I stammer, trying to find the perfect words, "Well, I'll just come out and say it, I'm donating a brilliant, smart, intelligent, AMAZING German Shepherd to the police

45

force today!!! Wow! Isn't that GREAT!?"

I hear a pause, and then a chuckle. "Yes, ma'am, yes, that's really nice. Ummm…"

I exhale a sigh of relief. Wow, this is much easier than I thought AND I'm doing a great deed. A great service to the mighty police.

"It's just that there is really no one who can talk you to about this right now, so why don't I take your name and your number…"

I pretend I don't hear him. "All I need is your address and I can have the dog there within twenty minutes."

He laughs again, "Like I said, Ma'am, there isn't anyone –

I cut him off, "I'm sorry, what's your name? I didn't get it."

"Weston," he replies.

"Umm hmm, Weston, let me be clear, I'm only right down the street and I'm on my way with the dog RIGHT NOW, so what's your address? I'd hate to leave her at the wrong spot as this is an opportunity of a lifetime."

"Okay, Ma'am like I said, we really appreciate this, but I need to have somebody else contact you regarding this."

"Somebody else?! Who!?"

Oh God, I'm raising my voice and becoming unwound. WESTON, I NEED TO DROP OFF THIS DOG NOW. NOT TOMORROW, CERTAINLY NOT MONDAY, BUT NOW! AS IN RIGHT NOW! RIGHT. FUCKING. NOW!

"What's your address?" I ask again meekly, hoping he will relent.

He does not.

He takes down my information and says someone will call me next week.

"Can I talk to someone else?" I quickly ask, but all I hear is him hanging up.

I get up, walk into my bedroom, and slam the door.

I get on my bed, peel down the covers, crawl underneath them, and I do something I haven't done in years and years. I start crying. As in long, painful, loud sobs.

I cry for Hollywood never making my movie, for the guy Noel, who never loved me, for my sister who lives right down the street and ignores me, for being stuck here in the South... for living in an overpriced apartment that I can't sleep in, and now I have a beast that I can't take care of.

Just another thing I'm failing at...

I cry and I cry and I cry and suddenly I hear someone scratching at the door.

Oh, no, not the dog.

The scratching gets louder.

Suddenly there's a BAMMMMMM!

THE DOG BREAKS INTO MY ROOM! She jumps on my bed and pins me down with her paws on my chest and stares right into my eyes.

I am startled by this.

My eyes open wide and stare into hers, and she does something in this moment that absolutely amazes me. She starts licking my tears.

She licks and licks and licks until I start smiling and my face is completely dry.

I sit up and stare at her.

She stares back at me.

And I realize that I have never had anybody comfort me before in my pain.

Every time I have ever cried, it has always been alone, with no one to even hand me a Kleenex.

47

It's like she's saying to me, "I've got you. Please just don't abandon me. I will do better."

I swallow, and realize how helpless she is.

I wrap my arms around her as if she is a life jacket and I kiss her face.

I kiss her and I kiss her until my heart is warm, and a small smile cracks on my face.

And this moment, bonds us for life.

Eleven

Chapter 11

I have to turn things around so I decide to make a list: Issues that need handling with the dog:
1. Get rid of scratching 2. Fix her food. 3. Potty training 4. Dog training 5. Fix her teeth.

Meg ended up chewing through my fan, my salt lamp, my Shiatsu machine, and now my space heater, (*but who's counting...*) so I decide to purchase a chemical treatment that I found online that's a weird apple flavor which deters the dog from chewing up any cords.

It's available at Petco, so I put Meg in the car wearing her new pink harness and seat belt that I just bought, clip her into the car, and together we take off.

Meg sits upright in the passenger seat like she's a back seat driver. She has a very serious expression on her face and she means business. It makes me giggle.

We arrive to the pet store and I buy a her new food, the sour apple spice chemical for the cords, beef raw hide chews, some toothpaste, and we enroll in Petco training for puppies. *We are on our way!*

After our successful excursion, I go home, feed her the new food, and we take a walk to the park afterwards for exercise.

When we arrive to the park, it's later than our usual time, and there's a very tall, strong looking woman there with her three dogs.

They're playing ball.

One of her dogs is huge; it is jet black and much bigger than Meg. The other is a medium sized brown lab, and her other dog is one of those weird, short, weiner dogs.

I watch them through the fence with Meg standing beside me.

The woman is maybe in her early sixties and she has total control of these dogs. She has a great arm and throws the ball far. Her dogs run, catch the ball, and promptly bring it back to her.

Why can't that be us? I think. *Why do we have so many problems?*

Meg and I stand there and watch from the sidelines.

When she sees us, she turns and waves, "Hi! Why don't you come in and join us?"

"That's okay. We will just watch," I reply.

I have no idea how Meg would get along with those other dogs, and I don't want to subject her to getting crushed by the big dog.

"Come on!" she repeats. "We can use the company!"

"That's okay," I state, and lamely stand there.

I have an immediate respect for this woman watching her with these dogs, and I know nothing about her.

One of her dogs wears a huge black vest that says, "Best Friend."

"Is that a service dog?" I ask.

I'm still standing behind the fence with Meg, looking like a loser.

"No! These are pound dogs!" she says. "Pound dogs!" she repeats, as if asking if they're highly professional trained dogs is the stupidest question on earth.

"Really?" I ask, surprised. "So is mine. I just got her from a shelter."

"Great! Come on in, join us!"

"Really? I don't know…"

I look down at Meg and she's staring at the dogs through the fence with wondering eyes, not barking or moving.

"Meg, do you want to go and play with those dogs?"

She gives me a look that says, HELL YES, so we go in.

At the park entrance, I hesitantly open the gate, unclip Meg's leash, and watch her take off after the dogs.

"Thank you," I say to this woman as I approach, "Wow, your dogs are really good with that ball."

She nods. She throws the ball again and Meg does a great job keeping up with her dogs.

I'm impressed. It's a small step, but somehow, it feels really huge.

"This is good," the woman tells me. "She's young and should be socialized."

I nod. "Yes, that's what the vet said. How old are your dogs?"

"Well, that one," she says, pointing to the larger dog with the vest, "is Zohan. He's my son's dog and he's in the air force so I'm watching him."

"Oh wow! Thank your son for his service. I love the name,

Zohan! How about the others?"

"The middle one is Lucy Goosey, and that other one is Osita," she says pointing to the hot dog bun.

I laugh. I love the dogs and I love their names. "I'm Juliana. What's your name?

"Pixie."

"Nice to meet you, Pix," and as I stand beside her, I admit, "You know, I am having some trouble with the dog. It's just not easy for me. I never cared for anything in my life other than a cat I once had, and this is really different for me, and well – I just don't think I'm doing a good job."

"Sure you are!" she says. "The dog is lucky to have you! You rescued a dog! Good on ya," she repeats. "Good on ya!"

"Yeah," I mutter, "Good on me," and I try to smile.

"You're doing great! Really, you are! Just keep at it!" she tells me. "It was hard for me too. It's hard for everybody! My dog Lucy Goosey has many behavioral problems. But they'll get worked out. I just hired a trainer for her."

I watch as she bends down and picks up the multiple bags of dog turd lying next to her. "Well, we have to get going, have a nice day!"

"Okay," I reply, "thank you, you too."

I watch as she leaves the park and I wish she had more time to stay with me.

I could really use a friend, and she was so nice.

Meg and I leave a short time later and when we get home, Meg is tired and had a really good time playing with the dogs, and my cell phone is ringing.

I rush to grab it.

Maybe it's Hollywood. "Hello?"

"This is the police department looking for Juliana."

I suck in my breath. I don't remember leaving my phone number with the police, and if I did, I didn't think they'd call.

Should I move forward with said plan? Do I want to give away Meg?

"Oh, hi," I say, slowly.

"Did you call?" she asks again, sternly. Her voice is harsh and mean.

"I did, yes," I say, stalling, looking for time.

Give her away, one side of me says.

Give her a better life. Devote her to the police force! The other says, things are getting better. We are getting along. She's a lot of fun. *Sort of.*

She's a lot of work, my other side argues. I don't even think she likes me. She gives me weird looks all the time, and probably hates this apartment lifestyle as much as I do.

"Well… I have some really fantastic news!" I coo.

I need to move forward with the plan. I need to move on with my life, and lugging around this German Shepherd is not a good long term plan.

Yes, get rid of her! Now!! NOW!!! "I have a fantastic German Shepherd that I'm donating to the police department! Isn't that fantastic!?! I can bring her by right now! What's your address?"

"Woah, woah, whoahhh!" she admonishes. "Back it up, sista! What?! A German Shepherd?"

I can't tell if she's excited or mad. "Yes! A big, wonderful, smart, fast, German Shepherd! Her sense of smell is incredible and I'm sure she can join the drug unit or the rescue unit, any unit!!" I hear my own voice and am feeling as ridiculous as I sound.

There's a long pause.

Maybe there's a chance, I think, *she's going to take this dog off my hands.*

Yet I wonder, is this what I really want? *To give her away?* Wouldn't she have a better life with me?

I DON'T KNOW!!!!

But I hear the policewoman say, very loudly, and very slowly, "So What. You're. Saying. Is: You adopted a dog and you don't want it anymore and you want to pawn it off on US?!"

I practically laugh out loud. Talk about being called out on your own b.s.

"NO!" I stammer. "I am not saying that at all! I am just doing my good service…"

She cuts me off. "Bub-bye, we can't take your dog," and she hangs up.

I look down at Meg who's looking up at me. I feel guilty. I smile at her. "What?" I ask. "I love you! I really do."

To make up for my almost mistake of "pawning her off," I take out her beef rawhide treat. "Look what I got…"

Twelve

Chapter 12

The next week, out come some small miracles. And by small, I mean turds - completed OUTSIDE! *Yes, that's right!*

We wake up, I leash her up, grab her treats, take her downstairs to her usual spot, and first she does a wee wee, and then as I stand there and watch, the circles begin, and she keeps circling and BINGO! She SHITS or is it SHAT!? ALL OVER THE GROUND!

"Yayyyyyyy!!!!!" I shout at 7 am, hardly caring if I'm disturbing the entire apartment complex. "You did it!!!"

I start jumping up and down. "Good girl, Meggie, good girrrrrrrrrrrl!!!!!!"

I pat her head as I read that's what I'm supposed to do as well as shower her with praise, and I'm showering. "Oh, my darling, I'm soooooo proud of you!!!!!!!"

The new salmon food seems to be working; the turds are

like perfectly formed brown logs, and they're not oily or runny. They're PURRRRFECT!!!

I happily pick them up with the plastic bag, discard them in one of the turd stations lying around the complex, and we head out for the park with a spring in our step.

The weather is warming up; it's now February, and as I sit in the lone chair in the park and throw Meg the ball, I am hoping that nice woman, Pixie, will arrive.

I notice that she comes to the park every morning at 8 am, so I've been trying to get here at the same time.

She has been a real rock in helping me with the dog. She not only has three dogs, I've also learned that she's a widow, has three children; one with a disability, and she works full time at a law firm. The woman is incredible.

Me, I can hardly handle ONE DOG without cracking and completely losing my mind.

I throw the ball and Meg returns it, staring up at me with her big brown eyes, but she likes to hog it before she'll give it back to me again.

"I love you, darling. Please give me the ball, come on," I urge, but she still hogs it.

I turn and see Pixie barreling around the corner in her large gray SUV, and Meg runs toward the fence to look out for Zohan.

She has come to enjoy her time with these dogs and I think she has developed a crush on the mighty Zohan.

"Is that your boyfriend, Zohan?" I ask. "Huh, Meggie?" I ask, laughing, "is that your new boyfriend?"

I get up off the chair to help Lizzie, and I open the gate for her dogs.

Her dogs come flying out of the back of her SUV, excited and barking up a storm. I've noticed that Meg has never barked yet.

Not one time.

Ever.

I sort have been wondering why.

Is she a mute? Why doesn't she bark like all the other dogs?

Pixie's dogs see Meg and rush for the gate door where we're standing, and when Pixie unleashes them, they flood inside.

It's a chaotic moment and fun, and Pixie always remains as calm as a goat. "Hiiiii Pixie, you look so pretty! How are you?"

The woman is so stoic, I have never heard her once complain. *About anything.* Yet she listens to mine ad nauseam.

"I'm fine," she says, "Just fine," and she keeps one eye on all her dogs.

She's on a tight schedule because of her job. "Osita already went this morning," she tells me, "but I need to wait for Lucy and Zohan."

"Good," I respond, and as I throw the ball, all four dogs take off after it. "Beautiful day, isn't it? Meg is potty trained," I drop on her.

"Oh, great! Really!?"

"Yep. Mission accomplished. That new food is working like a charm."

Pixie takes over the ball throwing from here since she can throw it much farther, and I resume relaxing in the chair.

Again Pixie picks up all the dog turds using only one bag, "I like to conserve the plastic, you know," she tells me, "for the environment."

I nod. The woman is *Rambo. Rambo, I tell you!!*

"So what do you have going on today?" I ask.

She goes through her long day with me, and I am always

amazed at her routine: morning aerobics, drop off her disabled child to work, and then she goes to work at a law firm. She works a full day, then back home to make dinner and then child activities during the evenings. After that, she has to walk all the dogs again.

Pixie also has memberships at yacht clubs and she's involved in neighborhood book clubs as well.

I wish she would invite me, but she hasn't done so yet and I think it's because of all my complaining about the apartment complex, my sister ignoring me, and all the trouble with the dog.

"Anyhow, I left another message for my sister," I tell her, "and still no call back. Can you believe it?"

She shakes her head.

"I mean, I don't get it. My only sibling, I live right down the road from her and NOTHING!"

She keeps throwing the ball.

"I'll guess I'll be spending all the holidays alone," I add.

"You're parents are up in Connecticut?" she questions.

"Yep, and I'm not driving up there… it's just too much with the dog, and I'm not a fan of long road trips or driving anyway."

"Well, at least you have her," she says, always finding the silver lining in everything.

Her words stay with me. *Yes, at least I have Meg.*

Meg and I leave after Pixie goes to work, and we walk around the lake and after I brush her. Meg loves being brushed, and so much of her hair comes off. "Spa treatment, darling. You are so beautiful," I whisper in her ear as I brush her long coat.

After she does more turds, we go home so she can eat and we can rest.

I watch CNBC and try to make money to no avail.

The market is ramping higher, I just keep averaging down in my short position putting everything on credit cards, including the rent, and it has been a long, losing battle.

I'm not sure I can sustain myself at these levels for much longer.

Hollywood isn't answering my emails, my books don't earn enough income, the rent is too high, and there's just not enough money coming in. I'm going to implode if things don't change soon.

I look at Meg.

She's staring out the window watching all the people leaving for work. And then she does something for the first time:

She barks.

Thirteen

Chapter 13

We embrace our first dog training later that evening at Petco. I didn't wake up in the best mood, which is hardly unusual since they "Upgraded the key fob," to our building, and the slamming door seems like it's getting louder, and sleep is virtually impossible.

The door slamming wakes me up numerous times per night, and I can't stand it. Plus, every time I am woken up, I feel the pain of my arthritis and can't fall back to sleep.

I take the dog and march across the apartment complex to pay the management team a little visit.

As we walk, I look down at Meg, and she's wearing her cute pink vest over her jet black coat, and she looks regal. Anyone who walks with a German Shepherd demands power. That's right, beside me is the most powerful dog on earth. The one depicted in books and movies as heroes; the ones police forces use as their guiding light.

60

Meg is strong, intelligent, powerful. She can run faster than anything I'd ever seen. Her sense of smell is impeccable; she'll always lead us right home to our doorstep with her in the lead and no guidance from me.

Crossing the parking lot, I notice all the people staring at us. I have always been beautiful but now with Meg, I am usually dressed in sneakers and a baseball cap because it takes brute force to control her, and we are still always stared at.

I can't imagine wearing a dress and heals, and having her on the leash beside me. Then we'd really stop traffic. That will perhaps take practice and training, hence the Petco lessons tonight.

But we are on the move now, and we ignore the stares and make our way into the Clubhouse.

I open the door and hold it for Meg, and she walks in first.

The management team looks up, and we stand there. We are a force; something not to be reckoned with.

I had already sent numerous emails out to corporate – numerous BLASTS of how disgruntled I am over the slamming door. They were not solving my problem and I needed help.

Now.

"Hiiiiiii," I begin, with the fakest smile I can muster. Meg stares at them. She is my silent but deadly dog beside me. Ruthlessly loyal, she can destroy anything in her path with just one look from me. Or so I like to think.

"Did you get my emails?" I chirp. "I was wondering when the door will get fixed. Now it's keeping my service dog up at night and she needs her sleep to do her job."

Blame it on Meg, I think. *Why should I be the Karen?*

The manager gets up and walks toward us.

Usually I dig into the containers of treats they keep on their desks for all the tenant's pets. But not today.

Today we mean business.

Stand back, I want to say. Do. Not. Come. Close. To. The. Dog.

Meg eyes them with her black eyes. Ruthless. Cunning.

"My dog is not happy," I add. "What's being done? Can we move apartments?" I ask, well knowing they won't. It costs them too much.

"Juliana, as we've told you before in the numerous emails that we sent to you, you are the only person complaining about the door."

"Because I am the only person living directly ABOVE IT!" I snap. "We can't sleep! People come and go at all hours of the night! Did you play the videos? My entire apartment SHAKES!"

"Juliana, we've adjusted the door as best we could. Now if you can just remember, we have the same key fobs installed on all of our doors at all of our buildings, and again, you are the only person complaining. We can break your lease. If you want to move, we understand...."

They're all staring at me.

I feel helpless.

I tried to move, but rents are so expensive everywhere and I just can't afford it. Plus, the prices movers are charging now since Covid where everybody is moving *somewhere,* is insane.

"I see you're not going to help me," I sneer. And then I use the line that my father told me to use in negotiations, "I will do what I have to do," I conclude, and Meg and I storm out.

We arrive to Petco and we're late.

There's only two other people in the class with their dogs. One is an overweight man with a little white fluff ball that looks like it cost him a million dollars, and another is a mom and son trio. The son has red hair, and beside him is his Lassie dog. I immediately like the trio. The son is adorable, and he's knelt down on the floor beside his big dog and he's overjoyed.

"This is Rubart," he announces as I sit down with Meg on the comfortable pillow I brought. Along with her water, her bowl, and her treats and toys.

"Hi Rubart, aren't you adorable?! You have a beautiful dog there."

"Thank you," he grins.

His mother smiles at me proudly.

I apologize for being late and the instructor begins with verifying the required paperwork. We need to show with proof of vaccinations, etc. etc., and then he starts rambling on about nothing.

I can hardly focus on the no sleep, and Meg has this look on her face like, "Is this over yet?"

She is sitting up warrior straight wondering what I got her involved in.

The instructor says we are going to walk our dogs around the store on the leash. *Really*, I'm wondering? Meg learned that on day 1. With no training.

We follow the group around the store doing laps down the aisles. People in the store stare at us strangely.

We look ridiculous, walking up and down the aisles with our dogs, so I use the time to look around at all the different toys and food, wondering how much more money I can blow on the beast.

I'm bored as high hell, and the instructor tells us, "When you turn to go down a different aisle, announce to the dog that you are 'TURNING,' so Meg and I blow down the aisles with me repeating, "TURNING, TURNING, TURNING!"

Meg is like, oh brother, shut the fuck up, and I spend the rest of the class alone with her in the training room taking selfies.

We quit the class after this, and get a full refund.

Our time will be better spent trying to CATCH UP ON OUR SLEEP, I think grimly.

Fourteen

Chapter 14

"I'm going to check out that over fifty-five elderly place in Daniel Island," I tell Pixie the next morning. "They're offering two months free rent and tonight they're having a clambake."

I've been searching for new apartments for weeks and I can't believe the inflated prices. Even in South Carolina!

I look at Pixie hopefully. She seems to have good intuition and I'm wondering if she thinks this is a good idea.

She doesn't say anything, she just keeps throwing the ball to the dogs.

"I mean, I know the deal Pixie, they get you in there and after a year, they jack up the rent... but maybe it'll work out for a year. I mean, I can't stand why I live now! I can't STAND IT! The slamming door, OH MY GOD! No sleep! Going on nine months now!"

"Really? You can't sleep? And you can't find any apartments

65

anywhere?"

"No! Pixie, they are expensive! I can't afford them! I've been looking for months. And even at $2,500 you're looking at places that are run down, on main roads, with loud air conditioning units that sit on your balcony…"

"Yeah, that's too bad."

I change the subject, realizing she has no idea of what I'm going through in apartment living. She lives in a big house. She doesn't have my kind of problems.

"How's it going with you? What's going on?"

We watch as Meg tackles Zohan down to the ground and pegs him there. "Meg!" I call. "Your MANNERS! Play nice!"

"Oh, let them be," Pixie says with a chuckle.

I can't help but also laugh because Zohan is so strong and so much bigger than Meg. I think she has a crush on him.

"Oh, same ol', same ol'. Drop my daughter off at work, then back to work for a project, and tonight we're going to a brewery with my daughter's bowling group."

I can't keep track of all her "groups." She seems to be a part of so many things. I longed for her life; her sweet office job where you can go and use somebody else's central air conditioning unit and sit in a cushiony chair, far away from the public, and get paid bank so you have money to actually do things in life or afford a decent place to live, and I'm secretly jealous that she lives in a big house.

How wonderful that must be, I think, *to have no shared walls.* No garage underneath you that jolts you away at three in the morning when the person who rents it decides to come home. Your own washing machine and dryer! Nobody living above you or below you blaring their music or cooking smelly food that seeps into your unit. And she has a full life; she's needed everywhere by everyone.

I have nothing.

Just Meg who depends on me completely.

Thank God for that.

Before we know it, Pixie is off to start her day, and I ask, "What time tomorrow, Pix? What time?" knowing it will most likely be the same time; 7:50 a.m. but she doesn't know she is the highlight of my day and my only friend.

"Yep," she says, "Same time, ten minutes to eight. Bye, have fun tonight."

Later that afternoon at exactly 1:00 pm, after watching my short positions take a bath in the market, I tell Meg, "Gang walk time!"

We put on our matching bandanas and I pack my pockets with crap bags, treats, keys, and her ball in case I need it, and we head out.

This is my favorite time of the day; the streets are usually quiet with most people off at work, and we take our time exploring the neighborhood.

Once we are out of the "luxury," apartment complex, we admire all the nice, little dollhouses. I tell myself I will be more patient with Meg today; that when she stops to sniff something, I won't be impatient; that I will find a way to stand there and pray, sing, or dance while she is enjoying her sniffing.

It can't be all about me," I tell myself. "We are a team, although I am supposed to be in charge. I am supposed to be the 'alpha male.'"

We walk and stop by the community pool in the next neighborhood.

I love to look inside the fence and admire the blue, sparkly water. I wish it were my pool and I could spend my day here swimming.

We move on, and Meg starts sniffing under a pile of leaves. I stand there and wait. By ten seconds, I get impatient. "Let's go, sweetheart." She keeps digging at something and I can see she is getting riled up.

"Honey, let's go," I repeat, as I look up at the sky, admiring the clouds and the sun, and the clearness of the day.

"Pouker, let's go," I say again, and gently pull on her lease, and when I look down at her, there's a massive dead squirrel in her mouth. "AHHHHHAHHHHHHHH!!!!!

I scream as loud as I can; and I am not a screamer, "AHHHHHAHHHHHHHH!!!!! AHHHHHHHHHHHHHH!!!! SOMEBODY HELP! HELP! HELP!!!!!"

Meg TAKES OFF down the street with the huge squirrel dangling from her mouth.

My screams echo down the empty roads. I am chasing after her down the middle of the street, calling "Help!!! Somebody help!"

We pass a group of landscapers who don't speak English, "My dog!!! She has a squirrel IN HER MOUTH!"

They shrug. They return to eating their lunch.

No help.

Meg is still running down the street and I chase after her, taking the ball out of my jacket and I throw it.

She drops the squirrel in the middle of the road, and chases after the ball. I catch up to her and grab a hold of her leash again, out of breath. "What happened?!" I ask. "What is GOING ON?!!"

Her tongue is hanging out and she is looking at me like, "What? What's you're problem, Mom? I'm just doing my dog

68

things."

I take her home, not sure if I should bring her to the vet or what.

I mean, do I really need another $200 vet bill? I call them as a precaution, and they tell me that she has her rabies shot and to just "Keep an eye on her."

We head over into the elderly place on Daniel Island later, and there's mounds of old people in line for the clambake by the pool when we arrive.

Meg and I walk in, and everyone turns to look at us. Somebody sneers, "Dogs are not allowed."

"This is a service dog," I reply, and I stand at the back of the line with Meg for some food.

I take a quick look around and see all the people dragging their oxygen tanks. People are giving us weird looks and seem snotty and mean, and by the time we get to the front of the food line with our plate, all the food is gone.

I'm disappointed, but I check out the studio apartments anyway with a sales agent, since it's all I can afford, and wonder what kind of life this will be for a German Shepherd and when I see it, it's just completely unlivable.

"This won't work for us," I tell the saleslady, finding comfort in the word "us," rather than me.

I am a part of a team, now, I tell myself. I have Meg. *But where do I fit in in the world?* I am too young for this. But I'm too old to deal with the loud late night pool parties they have at the other apartment complexes.

Where I live now, I am far away from the pool, I remind myself.

Maybe I should just stay where I am. It will save on moving costs. I'll just crank the noise machine louder, I tell myself, even though that doesn't work since it doesn't stop the entire jolting of my unit every time the front door downstairs slams.

When we get home, there's a large envelope at my door.

I turn it over, and see that it's from Josh, the property manager. It is a very formal looking package, and I open it up.

Inside, is a ten page legal document explaining the "Move Out Procedures," stating that they WILL NOT BE RENEWING MY LEASE.

"What?!" I read it over again, not believing my eyes.

Yes, it states VERY CLEARLY, they will NOT be renewing my lease. *Is this even legal?*

HOLY FUCK.

NOW WHAT?

Fifteen

Chapter 15

"They're EVICTING ME!" I tell Pixie the next morning. Pixie is still stewing from poor Lucy Goosey almost drowning or worse, getting eaten by the alligator in the lake across the street when her dog decided to go "for a swim," earlier.

I had to stand there hoping that the two big alligators who live in the pond didn't swallow her up, as Pixie stood behind me holding back her two other dogs.

For whatever reason, when all three dogs jumped out of her SUV that morning, Lucy Goosey ran straight for the deadly lake.

"Lucy! Come on!" I called, trying to rescue her. "WE LOVE YOU! COME BACK! Please Lucy!"

I could only see her little head and two front paws doing the doggie paddle, as she was taking a leisurely swim. "You're not supposed to be in there, Lucy," I add, as if she can understand

71

me. "Come on, girl, come back!"

I could feel Pixie's stress, and I couldn't even imagine what it would be like if the alligator swooped up and devoured adorable Lucy Goosey right before our eyes.

How did I even get here, I wonder. How am I living in a place with alligators?

"Please, Lucy, come back!"

Finally, the dog swims toward me. "That's it, good girl! Come on, just a little more..."

She swam up to me, and I grabbed her leash, pulling her out of the water, saving the day.

I was so relieved for Pixie, who's plate is already full, and she doesn't need a dog funeral right now.

By the time we got into the park, we wasted ten precious minutes before Pixie needed to get to work.

She needs to get her dogs pooped and run so they can stay in her house without wrecking it until she returns home from work at 6 pm.

Again, as I watch her, I don't know how she does it.

"Pixie," I repeat, "They're EVICTING ME! Can you believe it?"

"They aren't evicting you," she says, "they just decided not to renew your lease."

"I am being forced to move. This would NEVER BE allowed in California!" I reply.

Oh God, why did I even leave anyway?!

I remember my friend saying, "Do you really want to give up your rent controlled apartment? Why not sublease it for a year to ensure living on the East Coast is the right decision?"

"No, no, no," I told her. "I'm done."

How I wish I listened.

To even have the option to go back would be great, but then again, I'm not sure I would go, even if I could. The place had PROBLEMS, politics ruined it. It was too unsafe. *Too unsafe, I remind myself.*

"Look, you're not happy in that apartment anyway. It's good they're forcing you out. Now you'll try harder to find a new place. How was the fifty-five plus place in Daniel Island? Did you go?"

I often tell her I'm going places but then end up not going because I'm too tired or I just don't want to deal with it.

It's no excuse but life is hard on NO SLEEP. "Yeah, yeah, I went. It was terrible."

That's all I say.

I don't mention the oxygen tanks or the bad vibe.

"That's it!" I say with enthusiasm. "You're right! I will look harder for apartments! I can't STAND WHERE I LIVE NOW!"

When Meg and I get home, I make a large pot of strong coffee, and I continue on the housing search.

Do I want to stay in South Carolina?

No.

Maybe I should go to Connecticut to be closer to my elderly parents who may need me.

At this my father calls, "Just stay where you are," he tells me, "I'll help you with the rent. You have a great deal over there."

"A great deal, DAD!? In this overpriced hell hole?! I can't stay! They're not renewing my lease."

There's a long pause. "What?"

"East Coast laws are terrible on tenants. They are all pro-landlord!"

My father should know this since he made bank renting out the various beachfront properties he owned. "Don't worry,

Dad, I'll figure it out."

I hang up and feel lost.

I know my father is trying to help me, but I don't want to rely on him for money.

The fact is, it's almost impossible for a person to live alone with this high cost of living. But partnering up with someone would be even worse. I'd rather be dead.

I just close my eyes, trying to forget everything, as Meg lies by my feet.

She's looking out the window, probably longing for better days.

It's hard apartment hunting with a dog, especially a German Shepherd because 1. Landlords don't like dogs and most don't accept big ones. Yet she's my service dog, so legally they have no choice and

2. Meg gets tired with all the stair climbing and the heat. She needs her water, her treats, and breaks, etc. and

3. Driving around hunting for dump apartments on my disability payments is exhausting, and pretty much, useless.

After we search the entire area over the next two weeks, we decide that come May 5, in two months, we are leaving this state.

Going where?

I don't know.

But we ain't staying here.

Sixteen

Chapter 16

I try to find Meg's leash but it's buried underneath all the boxes that I have packed up during the last two months.

I don't know which is worse, being on the road, or *preparing* to be on the road.

My shoulder is in pain and my knees are all bruised up because Meg TOOK OFF yesterday when her leash was wrapped around my arm and I went flying after she got spooked by a big dog barking.

I went airborne and crashed to the ground. It's a miracle I didn't land on my face, and I can tell Meg feels bad about it, so it's all water under the bridge now, but this is the worst time for this to possibly happen. I need every once of strength and energy to pack up and move again.

I just moved from LA to Florida, and then from Florida to South Carolina, and now I'm moving again from South Carolina, to, I guess, Connecticut; the state that I grew up in.

I'll give it a year, I tell myself. *I will be close to my elderly parents in case they need me.*

A half hour later, when Meg and I get to the dog park, I see Pixie coming out of her SUV.

I get up to greet her, telling her how adorable she looks in her yoga pants; she always looks so cute in her little outfits, and all the dogs run into the park and start to play.

I plop down in the chair to ease my pain from the one of many dog accidents, and I start to get emotional.

"Pixie, if it wasn't for you, I don't know if I would have lasted with the dog. That day, you welcomed us into this park to play with your three dogs and it socialized her. You helped me so much with all your advice and I want to thank you, and you know Pixie," I say, with tears in my eyes, "I hope you find your life partner. You have so much going for you and you have such a heavy load to carry, I just hope someone comes along and helps you and you can get through it together."

She looks down at me sitting in the chair, "A man is not the answer…"

Her words hang in the air. She keeps throwing the ball, and I watch Meg beat out all three of Pixie's dogs. She wins every time!

"Meg wins again!" I laugh, trying not to look like such a sappy weakling.

"Well, you're going to be fine," she says, as if knowing exactly what I need to hear in this moment. "Everything is going to work out, Juliana. You never liked it here. You never got things going again with your sister…"

My sister.

I cringe at the words. I remember how hard this move has been. How her or her husband didn't even offer to help me, or her teenage son. I remember how I invited them over to my apartment complex numerous times – to swim in the "luxury pool," or to have dinner on my "veranda," without even a returned phone call.

Words cannot describe the pain and agony I feel, and probably always will feel, over this.

All the pain from crashing and falling with Meg yesterday doesn't compare to the pain caused by my sister.

I don't say anything. I'm afraid if I talk, I'll start to cry.

But I start crying anyway. "Oh Pixie, I don't even know where I'm going…"

I take a Kleenex out of my jacket and blow my nose. "I mean I registered for a silent retreat for two weeks up in Massachusetts and that buys me some time, and it was cheap, and I'm grateful for my aunt who is the nun at the convent in Connecticut, and she said she can take us in for a while… but I don't know if Connecticut is the answer."

"Just go and see," she says. "And take it from there. One foot in front of the other."

"Yeah… I guess you're right." I'm starting to wish I didn't have to leave. Meg and I have gotten into a routine. *Why couldn't I just find an AFFORDABLE APARTMENT where I can sleep?!*

Is that too much to ask?

The universe is pushing me in a different direction, my conscious argues. But I've been pushed, I want to argue back, all around the country.

I JUST WANT TO LIVE. I want to write. I want to go to the beach and relax. I want Meg to have a nice life and a decent home.

"What time are the movers coming tomorrow?" I hear Pixie

ask.

"...10:30."

"Good. So I'll see you here tomorrow, same time, okay? You hang in there. Everything is going to be okay," she says again, and starts to pack up her dogs.

I wasn't planning on coming to the park tomorrow; I have too much to do.

I thought today was going to be the last day I would see Pixie and her trio of dogs.

"Pixie, I don't think I can make it tomorrow..."

She cuts me off. "Meg needs to run! You have a long car ride ahead of you this week, so let the dog run off the steam tomorrow morning."

I watch Meg as she tackles Zohan and she's having a ball. I wonder if she knows these are our final hours here.

"Okay," I reply. "You're right, I'll see you tomorrow."

We put the leashes back on the dogs, and head out.

The rest of my day is spent closing down utility bills, changing mailing addresses, and returning the cable box back to the store, the same way I just did in Florida and California, and when I get home, there's no food because why bother; we're leaving, and I'm starving and exhausted.

I have no idea how all my stuff is going to fit into the "Pod," I ordered, but it was all I could afford.

It cost me five grand to move to Florida, and another five grand to move here from Florida.

My credit cards are ballooning out of control and I had to find a cheaper alternative than full fledged movers.

I went downtown to try to research Uhaul's but after sitting inside of one, I realized there was no way I could actually drive one, so I settled on the pod.

I planned to throw my bed out which I loved, but figured it could be replaced, and it was ten years old anyhow.

Meanwhile I have furniture and clothes and my computer that all needs to get jammed inside of something that's no bigger than a port o'toilet.

I don't feel that any of this is going to go well, but when the movers come the next morning, they are timely and fast.

They get the job done, everything fits into the pod, and the only problem I run into is my plants.

My big beautiful plants that I have been lugging around since I left LA couldn't fit into my car. I would have to leave them by the side of the garbage bin with all the other trash.

Just as I am dragging the plants over with Meg beside me, a girl pulls up in her truck. She rolls down her window and says, "You're not throwing those beautiful plants away, are you?"

I nod. "I can't take them with me. It's either the plants or the dog food." I want to break down and cry.

"I'll take them!" she says. "I'll give them a good home, I promise!"

"Oh, fantastic, thank you!"

It's a sign. My plants are saved. I take some photos of them, and then I watch her drive off with them.

Meg and I get into the car, "Are you ready, honey?"

I remember the peanuts that Pixie gave me earlier in the morning as well as a very expensive pair of yoga pants she got for me for the silent retreat. It was a goodbye present and so nice of her.

I put the peanuts beside me in the car, realizing how she was such a light to have come into my life just at the right time. I turn on the engine, and Meg and I start to roll out.

"Say goodbye, Meggie," I say, as she rides shotgun beside me,
"We are leaving this place. Bye!!!"
And off we go!

Seventeen

Chapter 17

❧❧❧

It seems to take forever to get out of South Carolina, but once I see the signs saying, "Welcome to North Carolina," I feel relieved.

It's over.

I turn to Meg and she's curled up in the passenger seat taking a nap. It's as if she knows that we're on the highway and she straps herself in for the ride.

I think about everything this journey brought me and didn't bring me. It's been almost two years since I left LA, and it's amazing what some time and rejection can do to a person.

When I first arrived to Florida, I was tan, excited and hopeful. I looked great and felt even better. I arrived with that "California sparkle."

Yes, I didn't get exactly what I wanted out of California; my movie wasn't made, but I had two published books that were selling, and I thought that would give me a better chance for the film.

Since Covid, the world has turned more "global," and "remote," anyway, and you didn't have to be in LA anymore.

Plus, the movie industry has undergone massive changes. Most films weren't made there anymore, so I felt good about my decision to go to the East coast.

Plus, I would get that one question answered that played on my mind for last twenty-five years, *What was He like now?*

Noel.

We were texting while I was still living in California. He knew about the book and he had bought it. Other traders bought it also and were writing me, telling me how good it was. I thought it would only be a matter of time, until He read it and then he would see how strong my feelings were for him back then.

Back then... the best days of our lives.

In our twenties, we were both working in finance during the dot.com bubble. Money, booze, the 1%, parties galore, private events with major headline artists like Stevie Nicks and Don Henley. The best of food, limousines, travel. It was off the hook, every second of it, and we were at the center of it. I lived to be with him. I loved him.

And that was the story of HEDGED. In great, glorious detail.

But when I got to Florida, all Noel would do was text me. He told me he broke up with girlfriend of ten years and left Tampa for Clearwater, Florida when I was right down the street in St. Petersburg.

The waiting was killing me; I was so excited to see him, but I had to get rolling with my life like getting a job and paying my new rent and all the debt since Covid. It was hard.

All of it.

First started with the broken refrigerator the landlord refused to fix. Then there was the neighbor underneath me who did nothing but smoke pot at all hours of the days and nights which seeped into my apartment, and when they finally moved out or were evicted, their cockroaches needed a new home, so they moved upstairs with me.

German cockroaches. *Everywhere.*

Nothing could get rid of these things. I had a full-time job now and I'm spending copious amounts of time hunting down exterminators to get rid of them. They even got into my bed. It was the worst, most traumatic thing I have EVER DEALT WITH.

I know illness and cancer is worse, but I went COMPLETELY OUT OF MY MIND living with these things.

After getting that under control, and after my mother blew into town ruining any hope I had with Noel because her rants caused me to take my frustration out on him, which I have since apologized for, but surprise surprise, the word "forgive," is not in his vocabulary so he ghosted me.

After he read the book, after he loved it, and after he was texting me all the time.

I didn't even do anything wrong to him. I was just ignoring him while I was going through problems with my parents.

I should have left then.

I should have just turned around and went straight back to Santa Monica.

But I stayed.

I stayed until they fired me at my new job selling Cyber security to hedge funds when I refused to make their SALES VIDEOS depicting my face and voice reading a script they devised and that would get sent out to thousands of potential clients over email. No thanks. Plus, I had no idea if this Cyber security even worked and they were poaching major accounts like banks and airlines.

I did not want to be the center of that if some big computer hack decided to break out. So when I lost my job, good luck finding another one in Florida because you can't. They hardly exist.

Jobs don't pay enough to pay the bills, and I just couldn't survive in Florida.

It was scam central. Everybody had their hand out looking for a payoff. The landlord took me to the cleaners, and when I came home the day before Christmas, I saw a three day eviction notice on my door.

It was all so surreal. What's worse was he got away with it. I didn't get evicted, but the judge told me I had to leave since it was now a precarious "situation."

My holidays were spent trying to find new housing while trying to lock in an investment banking job I had interviewed for which was like finding a canary in a coalmine in Florida.

After landing that job, it's hard to work when you're running around trying to secure more housing so they fired me, and then I left the state, all with NEVER GETTING TO SEE NOEL SHEFFIELD.

As if that wasn't all bad enough, when I drove up to South Carolina after not being able to find affordable housing in Vero Beach, I'm two weeks in and my sister decides not to invite me to my nephew's graduation for reasons unbeknownst to me, and when my parents and cousins flew into town, I got to stay home alone while everybody else attended both the graduation ceremony and after-party.

I was devastated.

Chapter 17

Driving farther and farther away, a sense of relief washes over me. I'm gone now, and it's in *the rearview.*

All of it.

I will never forgive my sister for living two miles down the road from me and ignoring me for over a year. Thanksgiving alone. Christmas alone. My birthday alone.

Had I known things were going to play out like this, I would have never left my rent-controlled apartment in Santa Monica, which yes, there were problems; the homeless and the antics from the "unhoused," were terrible, and it was dangerous, but it was nothing like these problems I'm experiencing *here.*

I drive for hours and hours, and it flies by in a haze, and when Meg and I arrive at a hotel off the highway somewhere between North Carolina and maybe even the next state above, I'm exhausted.

I check in, check out the room; it seems to be okay, then we go back downstairs to lug in our stuff.

Meg is a trooper, she doesn't bark, she doesn't complain, and she's right by my side.

I feel safe with her with me.

That's right, don't even try to come near us, she's a purebred German Shepherd.

She goes to the bathroom before we head in for the night, and when we get upstairs, I feed her and give her water.

I get two queen beds so she can sleep in the bed right beside me.

After playing with her ball and rubbing her belly for an hour, I fall asleep the second my head hits the pillow.

I hope that when I wake up in this new state of wherever I'm at, the universe decides to throw me a better hand of cards.

Eighteen

Chapter 18

I wake up in the hotel the next morning, not knowing exactly what state I'm in, and I'm not looking forward to the eight hours of driving ahead of me.

I look over at Meg and she's on the other bed, sleeping peacefully.

It gives me solace seeing her so at ease. She looks like a person, curled up, with her head on the pillow.

"Good morning, sunshine," I say, as she lifts her head. She is not a morning person and she stirs but stays still.

"Let's get it rolling," I add, and I roll into the shower. The shower is okay, typical hotel shower, but I am grossed out that they now replaced the little shampoo bottles with large pumps of which I have to touch, not knowing who touched those bottles before me and what condition their hands were in.

I jump out of the shower, find a hand towel and pump the

shampoo, and can't wait to get out of here.

It's a long pack up with the dog food and her toys and balls and leash, and vest, and all my stuff, and we finally make our way out to the car.

I stop by the hotel desk to get a printout of my bill, because I can't stand it when I don't, and then I check my credit card statement days or weeks later and find a bunch of wrong charges.

I can smell the breakfast and am debating if I should go in and grab something, but curiosity calls the cat, so after my belongings are safely in the car, I go back inside with Meg to see if there's anything good.

The worst thing a person can do, is to drag a German Shepherd around a morning buffet at a hotel breakfast.

Meg is trying to get her nose into everything and even though she has her "service vest," on, she is causing a stir, and pulling me. I try to act like I have everything under control as I stick a paper cup under the coffee spout.

It smells good and strong, and I douse it with sugar, all while trying to control Meg, and I wish someone would offer to hold her for a second and I refuse to leave her in the car because we are somewhere along some highway, and anybody could smash my window and take her, and that is my worst fear.

I look at the under cooked scrambled eggs, the gross looking muffins wrapped in plastic, and I grab a couple of boxed cereals and oatmeal packets for the road, and we get out of there.

I would love a cup of orange juice to take with me, but that would incorporate getting another cup and pouring it while holding the coffee and the dog.

Impossible.

We make our way out to the vehicle, I put Meg inside and we drive off.

Two hours in, I feel good. I only have had a sip of the coffee since I don't want to have to go to the bathroom, the radio is blaring and we veer off this main highway I-95 and head West where I can pick up a highway that goes North but it has more of a view.

Less trucks, my research told me. I find it easily, and we continue North. I love how the scenery changes from dry branches and grayness to the beautiful greenery and lushness of the trees in the North. Even the air starts to smell, cleaner, fresher.

Meg needs to use the bathroom, so I get off the highway somewhere, I think I'm in Virginia by this point, and I look for a park.

We find one, and Meg gets out and once we're securely in the center of it, I take off her leash so she can run.

We both do, and we are free. We are laughing, and running and chasing the ball. It feels so good to be out of the car and in the fresh air.

After she goes, we sit under a tree and just enjoy the air. A couple passes us holding hands and they look at Meg and I and smile.

"Do you know what state I am in right now?" I ask.

At first they think I am joking.

I am not one to tell people, "I am on the road," but with Meg, I feel somewhat safer, and at first they don't respond. "What?" they ask, confused.

"Is this Virginia?" I ask.

"You are in Maryland," they answer puzzled. "Where are you coming from?"

"South Carolina," I say, "This is nice, this park."

"Sure is," they agree, and it is. So peaceful and you would never guess the highway is right down the road.

Meg and I hit the road again and by 4 pm, I am tired. I am sick of driving and the air is hot, and we have no air conditioning in the car, and with the windows open the whole time, it's just a lot of noise on the highway, and I'm spent.

I find a hotel and go in with Meg.

"Is she a service dog?" the young woman asks.

"Yes, I have paperwork if you need to see it and she has her vest on," I reply, pointing to Meg who seems to be getting used to checking in and out of hotels and handles it in stride.

"How much for a room tonight?"

"One thirty plus tax."

"Okay, can I see the room before I check in?"

She tells me I have to pay first, and at this point, I know there is a Crackle Barrel down the road and I can just walk there with Meg, get her walk in, get food and come back and go to sleep. "That's fine," I say, and hand her the credit card.

The room is fine; no weird odor or vibe, looks clean and we make our way out.

Crackle Barrel is mayhem and I order up big; a cheeseburger for Meg and a grilled chicken sandwich for me.

When we get back to the room, I am juggling way too many things, the three little plants I did manage to save, they needed water, and Meg's dog food, and her bowl and my clothes and my pillow and blanket. I really loathed using hotel's pillows and their blankets.

We barrel inside, and by this point, I'm somewhat irritated and overwhelmed and knowing there is no end in sight to this until I secure housing, somewhere *anywhere*, and have no idea where this will be at this point, and knowing, given my budget, the pickings will be slim.

Very slim.

I get Meg settled with her water, and pour food in her bowl which she devours but she can smell something good is waiting and after a hot shower, and feeling better in clean sweatpants, a T-shirt, sweatshirt and thick socks, we jump into a bed and dig into our food.

There is something romantic about eating with Meg. She sits up straight and watches me eat, staring deeply into my eyes. She waits patiently as I share with her my food.

"Look at this, Meg, delicious."

She devours the hamburger and I take a bite of hers, and share with her my chicken sandwich, letting her have all the bacon.

She eats slowly, with purpose, and sniffs everything out thoroughly. I read that dogs taste with the nose, not their mouth and sometimes when I give her treats, I'll notice she'll take the treat and sit down with it on the floor, savoring it with her nose before she eats it.

It is a show. I am happy, she is happy, we are watching David Muir on the news and life seems great.

And then she turns to the door, it's now dark outside and she starts growling.

I have never heard her growl before in this manner. She stares at the door and this low pitch growl comes out of her mouth and she barks, low and fierce, just one bark. I turn down the TV and someone is trying to get into our room.

I can hear the door clicking and I freeze.

I glance at the table top that the TV rests on where my room key should be and I don't see it.

90

I get up and look in my purse and look around the room, and I don't see it anywhere!

In my confusion in entering the room earlier, carrying all my items, the large bag of food, and Meg, I must have dropped the key on the floor.

Oh my God!

I call downstairs and inform them to immediately please change my room key and I will be downstairs in the morning to pick it up, explaining what happened.

They do it, the door is bolted, always was bolted, and Meg calms down.

Dodged that bullet, "Good girl, Meg," I tell her, petting her head. So grateful I have this dog.

She's the best security on the planet.

Nineteen

Chapter 19

We leave early the next morning, the hotel doesn't have a free breakfast, and when Meg needs to use the bathroom, we stop off at a running river.

There's a picnic table and I sit down on top of it and watch Meg walk around at the water's edge.

It's beautiful and peaceful, and I'm happy to just be here alone, and someplace that's not in a car, or a hotel room, or walking alongside a highway hotel.

I can sit here for an hour, I think, listening to the running river, the sun on my face, and suddenly, this lone man gets out of his truck which is parked nearby and starts walking towards me. *Oh, damn.*

He comes over, he's like a chatty Kathy, asking me questions, telling me about his dead wife, and I don't know if it's a story he's made up or if he's just a lonely guy who's really just depressed over his dead wife, but I'm not one in the mood to take chances right now, so I grab Meg and tell him, "My boyfriend hates it when I'm late, we've got to go," and Meg and I abruptly leave the premises.

We take the scenic route through rural Pennsylvania and I never realized what an old-fashioned, historic area it is.

Driving through their Main Streets, I love observing the old time gas stations, pizza parlors, and egg stands. It's like taking a time out of the 1800's and it's slow paced and tranquil. There's rolling hills, cows, and so many large beautiful trees and flowers.

Once we pass through, we hit New Jersey and then New York.

I'm making good time, and things start to look familiar. When I catch I-95 back in Southern Connecticut, it occurs to me, that I'm home.

I sit in traffic and on the right is a huge mall that was never there before, and when I hit Westport, I veer off the highway and drive out toward Compo beach.

My father owned two houses on the beach there, and during high school, when my mother argued with me and my father, we would live there together, in those houses while I commuted to high school.

It's something to see those houses now; our old houses have been torn down and mini mansions exist here now.

It's as if an entire history has been wiped out, and new things are in their place, with new people living here.

I get out of my car, tears in my eyes, and I observe it all in awe.

I let Meg out, realizing she knows nothing of my life or history here. The childhood memories; Peter Frampton singing happy birthday on the beach to my old childhood dog, Chachi.

Westport was a beautiful, chic town. And one needs obscene wealth to live here now.

I speak to one of the neighbors who comes outside, "I used to live here," I choke, pointing to the house across the street. "Would it be okay if I leave my car here for a few minutes so I can show my dog the beach?"

He's nice, shakes his head, "Sure," and Meg and I take off.

It's wild watching Meg run in the waves. I walk alongside her on the beach with a heavy heart, not knowing what's going to come of this visit here or how long I will stay or how I will survive.

It's strange to be so close to my parents who live in the next town over, and to not be able to call my mother and have her tell me to come over.

I feel so alone, like a stranger in a strange town that's no longer home to me, but LA seems a million miles away and I have to just keep moving forward.

My plan is to stay with my aunt; my father's sister who's an elderly nun at the convent in Hamden, Ct. This is not the most ideal plan, but it's a plan, and we've always been close. She was always trying to escape the convent, but I guess her plans never panned out.

I have no idea which hotel I'm staying at tonight, and I know given the area I'm, I'll be paying a pretty penny.

I sit down on a bench in front of the boats and watch the water. Meg is beside me and she's wet and sandy from playing in the water.

I take her back to the car and dry her off. She could use a bath, and I could use a rest on a couch, any couch — but I don't have one.

94

Because now I'm technically homeless.

I move the car not to take advantage of that gentleman's generosity of allowing me to park in front of his home, and I stare out the window.

To think at fifty-six years old, all roads have led me here to this.

My mother has no idea I'm here and she doesn't care. She wouldn't take me in if my body was on fire.

And now, I feel as if there is no fire left inside me.

I get teary but I cannot start crying. Not with the dog right near me. She is in tune with my every feeling, and I must pretend that this is an epic adventure — that this is a fun trip and we're going to win it.

But I can't help it, the tears are coming and my heart is in pieces.

This is the moment in a movie known as "the dark night of the soul." It's when the character faces undue hardship and they can't see the way out.

Only this is not a movie I am writing.

This is me right now.

This is my life.

Twenty

Chapter 20

"Come here now!" my aunt in the convent says when I call her. I'm still parked on the side of the road and it's getting dark.

"Really?" I ask, "Are you sure I'm not imposing?"

"Of course not!"

"But Auntie Jo, I'm early and Sister Victoria says the room won't be ready until Friday."

"I'll go find Sister right now and check. Just call me back in ten minutes, okay? I'll look around for her and try to get you the key!"

"Okay, yes!" I reply, "Thank you! That would be wonderful!"

Oh, please let there be space for us at the convent.

I am in no mood to check into another hotel right now... or ever for that matter...

The phone rings, my aunt has the key, and says, "We're all set! How long will it take for you to get here?"

I plug her address into my phone's GPS, "Ninety minutes!"

"Great," I'll see you then!

"Oh, thank you, Auntie Jo! This is great! I can't wait to see you!"

"I can't wait to see you, too! Bye!"

I click off and start driving.

When I pull up to the convent, my aunt is waiting for me at the bottom of the hill.

I get out of the car, emotional, and wrap her in a big hug. "Hiiiiiii!!!" I've missed you so much!"

I look into her eyes, and it's like seeing my grandmother and grandfather combined. "You look great," I tell her. She looks older now, lots of gray hair, but she still has that spark.

"You too!" she exclaims.

She points to a tiny dollhouse at the top of the hill. "That's yours. That's where you'll be staying! I have the key and I'll meet you up there, okay?!"

"Yes, perfect! Thank you!"

"Thank you for coming! And who's this?" she asks, bending down to look in the car window.

"Oh, that's my little love bug, Meg."

"She's precious!"

"Thank you! It's been a long ride for her and …."

"I can imagine," my aunt replies, "Let's get you settled. Meet me up at the top of the hill by the stone house, okay?"

My car is packed wall to wall with my belongings, and I can't squeeze her inside. "Yes, perfect, thank you again."

As we drive through the grounds, the convent is set on a majestic hill, surrounding by trees, stone walls, and beautiful statues of Saints. The landscape is just as beautiful as I remembered, and I haven't been here in over thirty years.

At the top of the hill is a Catholic school, and on the side of the school is a plaque that's in honor of my grandfather's bother; my great uncle.

Seeing our family name makes me feel like I'm being welcomed home.

My aunt gets to the top of the hill, and she holds onto Meg while I gather my belongings and take them inside.

The place is adorned with every need imaginable; shampoo, soap, laundry machines, a full kitchen. It is spotlessly clean, and adorably warm and cozy. I am so happy.

She leaves to retrieve a hot meal for me from the main building.

After I take a hot shower and wash Meg off with some towels, my aunt drops off chicken parmigiana with pasta.

I share it with Meg after she leaves and food has never tasted so good.

I crawl into bed and plan to sleep like I've never slept before.

Two days away from South Carolina, and I already feel like I'm in a completely different world.

I fall into a deep, dark sleep, unawakened by anyone trying to break into my hotel room, any slamming doors, or trash compactors that rattle my room and my life.

I'm so grateful.

The worst is over, I think.

The worst has definitely *got to be over.*

Twenty-One

Chapter 21

꧁꧂

A t 5:30 AM, someone is ringing the doorbell. I wake up and look around, trying to remember where I am. I see the picturesque landscaping and greenery, and remember that I'm at the convent.

I have two windows in my room, one on each wall, and the cross breeze is refreshing. The air is clean and sweet, and I awake feeling rested. I hear the doorbell ring again, and realize I'm not dreaming.

Meg starts barking already on her guard duties, and I make my way downstairs to see who's at the door.

I'm so happy to see my aunt standing there, and I swing the door open.

She's dressed in her full nun clothes with a big smile on her face. "Am I too early?!" she asks. "Am I too early?"

"No, of course not!" I embrace her and kiss her.

Meg comes running down the stairs and joins us, the sun

beaming down on all three of us.

"How are you? How did you sleep?"

"Oh, excellent," I reply. "Thank you so much for allowing us to stay here. It is so beautiful."

Meg keeps barking and my Aunt Jo is not afraid of her; she just stares into Meg's deep brown eyes with her deep brown eyes, and Meg knows she's a force. Her perky dog ears are like radar dishes for my aunt's love.

"Is it too early?" she asks again.

"No! Not at all!"

"What time is it?"

"It's early," I say, "but no worries, come up for coffee... I just have to get the dog's leash and take her out."

"Oh, okay, okay."

We walk upstairs and I take off the blankets I put down on the couch for Meg so she wouldn't soil it.

"Sit down, relax."

"Yes, I had to get out of there," she reminds me. "Had to!"

"I understand," I reply, although I really don't. My aunt has been complaining she wants to escape the convent for years. I can't understand why she would want to leave; it's so peaceful and everything is done for her here.

"I'll take the dog out, you sit and watch TV, okay? I'll be right back."

I turn on the TV for her. "Oh, okay."

"Unless you want to come?" I ask. My aunt has been looking frail so I'm not sure she'd want to join us.

"No, that's okay, you go."

"Okay, perfect!"

I leash up the dog, put a hoodie jacket on and a fleece navy blue vest that I've had since I worked in investment banking.

It has the bank logo on it and the quality is second to none. It has big pockets so I can hold Meg's treats, balls, and doodie bags.

"I'll be back soon!"

Meg and I walk outside and the air feels great and we take off for the park down the hill. There I let Meg off the leash and we both run around.

After twenty minutes of playing ball with her, we head back up to the little stone house. I see my grandfather's brother's name again on the side of the school and remember what a good family I come from.

I feel honored to be a guest here, and somewhat at home.

"So how's it going?" I ask my aunt, when I get back inside.

I notice that the dog is waiting for her food and my aunt is waiting for her coffee, and it is time for me to wait on everybody.

"Good, do you want me to do anything?" she asks.

"No, relax. I have some oatmeal and I'll make us that for breakfast along with some hot coffee, okay?" I ask.

"Sounds great," she says.

It comes to my realization, that she is in fact, incapable of making coffee or doing anything which saddens me. Her dementia is much worse than I had perceived.

I pour the dog some food and fill the Keurig machine with hot water, and I make the oatmeal.

We sit down together and say a prayer over our hot breakfast. She forgot how to say Grace, so I say it for us.

We start to eat, and I'm so glad I remembered to bring the oatmeal packets; it will be enough to sustain us for the next couple of days. I have no plans of getting back in the car anytime soon.

"This is so incredible, Auntie Jo. Thank you so much for taking us in. So how you? How are things?"

"No, there's been a change here. A very big change. And I just, how do I say it? I don't like how they are doing things here."

"How so?" I ask.

"Huh?"

"How are they doing it?"

"What do you mean?" she asks.

"You just said everything is different now, how?"

"Oh, I forgot. I'm sorry! I forgot what I was saying."

"That's okay," I reply, sipping the hot coffee and dousing it with more sugar packets. "How do you feel?"

"Oh, I feel great! Dr. Sun, she says..."

I watch my aunt and she turns to look out the window.

She stops speaking.

We are sitting at a little table that's flooded with sunlight as it sits underneath a tiny greenhouse. She has a far away look on her face. "Dr. Sun says what?"

"Who?"

"Dr. Sun."

"Who?"

"What did Dr. Sun say?" I ask.

"Oh. I don't know."

I stare at her. My heart drops.

Her face gets sad. "I guess I don't remember what I'm saying," she admits.

I grab her hand across the table and squeeze it. "It's okay. I love you. That's all that matters."

I look over at Meg for some relief. She's sitting on the floor between us like a third wheel, listening to our conversation.

"And I love her, too," I add, smiling.

My aunt looks down at the dog and grins. "She is beautiful."

"I know. She's a dreamboat."

For the next few days, the three of us get into a routine. My aunt comes over every morning at the crack of dawn and wakes us all up, and then I take care of the dog, make us breakfast, and my aunt returns to the convent for her lunch. After that, I shower and watch the market and try to make some money to no avail.

We all meet up around four o'clock for some dinner. I usually drum up something in the little kitchen using the pans I brought along with some cans of soup. It's not much but it's enough.

By the fifth day, I'm starving and we have to make it out into the real world for some real food.

There's an Italian deli down the street, and I remember my aunt taking me there when she was well and she could drive. We order a steak sub with mushrooms and cheese, a turkey sandwich with the works, and a spinach calzone over the phone.

I unload some more of my items out of the car, get my aunt and the dog into it, and we take a nice drive down there.

We bring the food home and all three of us enjoy it. It's fresh, hot and delicious, and to finally eat real protein, I feel satiated.

We make plans to get together with my parents the following week at Crackle Barrel in Milford, Connecticut, which is a middle ground for all of us.

They will be meeting Meg for the first time.

"Can you believe my mother wouldn't take me in?" I ask my aunt again, as I take another bite of the steak sandwich.

"To this day, I have no idea what I did that was so rotten that makes her loathe me so much."

"She hasn't changed," she replies, wiping her mouth with a napkin.

My Aunt seems has forgotten so much, but she remembers my mother very clearly.

"And my sister," I add, "How could she ignore me for an entire year when I lived right down the road from her?" I ask, in disbelief.

"I'm surprised. It just doesn't sound like her at all."

"I know! It's her husband," I proclaim. "I don't know why she married him!"

My aunt stares at me across the table. It's like she wants to say something but she can't find the words.

I wait but nothing comes out.

And then she says, "Your mother, when she was young and she first met your father, my brother," she says with a distant voice. "Your mother was so beautiful. She was so different, then, so … happy."

I nod.

I remember seeing all the photos of my mother when she was young. She was beautiful and looked just like Jacqueline Kennedy. Her hair was always coiffed in a massive bun on top of her head and she had tailored clothes. She was always smiling and had perfect white teeth. "What happened to her?" I ask.

My Aunt looks at me for a moment.

"When did it all change?" I push.

My aunt turns to look out the window again.

And then, in a lucid moment, she replies, "When she had you."

Twenty-Two

Chapter 22

The next few days I keep my head down and relax with the dog at the convent. We find a quiet solace there, and I love spending time with my aunt.

We walk the beautiful grounds, admiring the spiritual statues that line the grounds, as I stop to observe one. It reads:

"At the end of the sorrowful journey,
You will be permitted to look backward;
then you will see with joyful astonishment,
The furrow you dug with such pain,
All blossoming behind you."
— Mother Clelia Merloni

The convent was founded by Mother Clelia and I also spent time reading her biographies that were left around the little stone house. She has a fascinating story; she was creative and passionate and was destined to follow her father into the business world, but instead chose the religious path. Her philosophy was "others," just like my grandfather and my aunt, and I couldn't help but wonder, if she was living in today's world, would she still feel the same?

I think this is what my aunt meant by wanting to escape the convent. She wanted to be on the streets helping people. But the streets seem so rough now.

We keep walking, and I love staying up here in this insulated world, and if I had my way, I would never leave.

Hell soon resurfaces, as by the end of the week, we're slated to meet my parents and relatives on my mom's side at Crackle Barrel off the highway in Milford.

Though I'm excited to see my father, I find myself nervous, and I dress accordingly.

I take time applying my makeup, and I wear a nice white sweater with a Tommy Hilfiger crew underneath and my Investment Banking navy blue fleece vest over that since it's cold.

When I get my aunt into the car along with the dog, she keeps asking, "Where are we going? Where are we going?" even though I've told her a thousand times about this lunch.

"We're going to have a fantastic lunch!" I promise her. "You're going to see your brother, Jerry."

"Who?"

"You're brother, Jerry."

"Who?"

"Jerry!"

We start to drive off and I am grateful for the comfortability of my car. It's like my second home.

There's no air conditioning, and my aunt starts complaining that it's too hot. "It's hot, I'm hot…"

"I know," I tell her, "I'm sorry. The AC is broke."

We're all broken, I think, ready to withstand my family's judgment today.

After finding the restaurant a long hour later, I pull into a parking space and my father pulls in right beside me.

I look out the window and see my mother.

My heart drops.

I'm filled with an anxiety and an insecurity that I cannot describe.

My Dad's Mercedes is black, and it's a beautiful sedan and they exit looking perfectly coiffed.

Me and my aunt get out of the car, looking like we've been through a hurricane. Our hair is blown all over from the windows being open.

"Hi Mom," I say, as I let the dog out.

I reach for my father first and hug him. He and I are close; I don't need to put on a show.

But with my mother it's different. "How are you, Mom?" I ask, "This is Meg."

My mother starts laughing at the dog. She comes prepared with treats and shoves them in the dog's face.

Meg is trying to smell her, and I try to pull Meg away.

My mother takes an immediate disliking to the dog when the dog sniffs between her legs. "What is she doing, Julie? Have her stop!"

"Meg! Meg!"

I remember my aunt is with me and try to fold her into the conversation. "Auntie Jo has been so good to us, she has taken us in and provided us with a great home until we get settled."

Unlike you, mom, I want to say, *who wouldn't even let me come over once.*

But I don't say that.

I can't.

My father is waiting for an argument to ensue, and I can't afford one now. I'm like a ship without an anchor, and now I have this dog to lug around.

Every move I make must be perfectly orchestrated.

Or else *I will* be living in my car with the dog.

We make our way inside the restaurant, and I feel uncomfortable walking in with this huge German Shepherd, and it's packed.

I explain that she's my service dog, and Meg is fine for the first ten minutes as she sits under the table, and munches on her beef rawhide that I brought.

The rest of my family is already seated and they begin complaining that we're late, and the elephant lies in the center of the room, that "Julie is home and Julie doesn't have housing or a man or a job. She is now disabled and has a dog. She failed in LA, obviously, and she should have been more like us – stayed in Connecticut their whole life."

They don't say this, but it's the vibe.

Meg starts getting antsy, and it's a good excuse for me to leave, and we walk outside.

We walk through the restaurant avoiding the stares, and when we get out, I look toward the highway and watch all the cars go by.

I was once on that highway on the road to no where, and soon I will be on it again when my time is up at the convent, as I'm heading to a two week silent retreat with the dog in Massachusetts.

I'm looking forward to the silence. I just hope that the voices in my head stop.

My father comes out of the restaurant and finds me.

I am carrying around Meg's crapola in a doggie bag, and I'm looking around for a trash barrel. "Oh, hi, Dad!" I say.

"You didn't eat anything," he says.

"That's okay, I ate," I reply. The food was nasty and I have no appetite anyway.

"So what are you going to do? What's the plan?" he asks.

"I don't know, Dad." The cars are zooming by. I have no idea why we came to this restaurant, and I can't wait to get out of here.

"What?" he asks over the blaring traffic.

"I don't know, Dad. I'm hoping for a market crash by the time the silent retreat gets out so I can get some money and rent something. And I'm hoping, that the housing market implodes with it so I can find something that's affordable."

"Where?"

"I don't know."

I want him to say, "Ridgefield," which is the beautiful town he lives in and where I grew up, in Fairfield county. But it'll never happen.

I'm here only for you and Mom, Dad. I want to be close to you in case you need me. I mean you're in your eighties. Isn't that what people my age are supposed to do? Come home and take care of their parents? Or am I just supposed to stay out in California and let you rot?

But my mother wants nothing to do with me. We all know that. And my father is caught between us.

I wish he would just agree with me, that this journey from Florida through South Carolina and now up to Connecticut has been a complete wash; that my mother never warmed to the idea that I'm home, and she'd rather see me back in California and honestly, I wish that after all this, I never came.

In fact, I'd give anything to go back. But how? With the dog, I'd have to drive now?

And the cost... *oh God, the cost...*

It'll never happen. Not now.

I'm stuck.

I'm stuck and everybody knows it.

We leave and I can't wait to just huddle up and be alone again, and in a few days, Meg and I are on the road again heading to Massachusetts.

And hopefully, the two week silent retreat will provide some clarity.

Twenty-Three

Chapter 23

❧

"**D**oes any of this look familiar?" I ask my Aunt Jo, as we drive around in circles trying to get to the beach in Branford, Ct.

"Familiar? Oh, I don't know."

"Do you recognize we're in Uncle Freddy's neighborhood? By the beach?"

"Who?"

"Uncle Freddy, your brother."

"Who?"

"Uncle Freddy!"

"Oh…I … don't know."

I'm due to leave for the meditation retreat tomorrow, but I promised I'd take my aunt to the beach before I left.

Meg is sitting in the backseat staring out the window. I'm trying to find my uncle's old apartment for my aunt. "We're going to pay homage to Uncle Freddy today? Okay?"

"Freddy? Who's that?"

"Your brother. Your brother Fred."

She nursed my poor uncle to his death when he was diagnosed with prostate cancer five years ago.

Maybe it's better she doesn't remember anything at all, I think.

"Don't worry, there it is," I say, pointing to his old apartment complex and driving into the parking lot.

My uncle lived by the beach on the shoreline in Connecticut when my aunt hooked him up in some affordable housing complex.

My aunt aunt ran three convents in three different states when she was well, and was she principal of one of the most prestigious Catholic schools in the world. It's a shame what dementia does to people.

"We're here!" I say, relieved I found it. "We're going to pay homage to Uncle Freddy by going by his old apartment."

My aunt is silent as I let her out of the car. I open the back door for Meg, and unhook her seat belt and she jumps out.

I turn back to my aunt, and she's looking all around. Suddenly, something magical happens.

"Does it look familiar now?" I ask.

And her face lights up. "Yes...." And she remembers.

"Looks like you're remembering Uncle Fred now! Huh?! This was his old place..."

We walk around the grounds and my aunt is in awe. She's silent, just taking everything in.

"You helped him, you did everything for him, Auntie Jo. He is now watching us and protecting us from Heaven."

She nods.

Meg finds a dead mouse and starts to sniff it. I yank her

112

chain. "Let's go sweetheart," I tell her as we circle the grounds.

"So pretty here," I say. And it is.

It is a cute apartment complex and although a bit run down, I remember my uncle being pretty happy here.

As we circle the building and I'm trying to get a quick walk in for Meg, my aunt walks over to somebody's door. I turn to see what she's doing and she starts to knock. The door opens instantly, and a very old woman steps out.

"Hello?" she asks.

And my aunt, my suddenly very lucid aunt says to her, "Hi, do you remember me? I'm Sister Jo Ann. My brother was your neighbor."

The older woman wraps my aunt in a huge hug. "Oh my God! Sister Jo Ann! How are you?!"

I watch and cannot believe it.

We're invited inside, and I stay with one foot out the door so Meg doesn't go in.

"Oh, your brother Fred, he was so good," Angie says.

My aunt nods. I can see some tears in her eyes. "This is Angie," she says to me, and introduces us.

"Hi Angie," I say, and I like this woman already, she's a bright white light.

"I'm ninety-three years old," she informs me.

"Wow," I say, "God bless you. You look wonderful."

"Sit, sit," Angie tells my aunt, and Meg is pulling me so I excuse myself.

When I come back inside a few minutes later, my aunt looks up at me. "Angie says there's an apartment available here. Maybe you can have it."

"What?! Really?!" I ask, not believing my luck. "Do you know how much it would cost? I'm on disability now, and my income is limited."

"That's perfect!" Angie says, "That means you'll meet the income requirements. Oh, I would love to have you as my new neighbor."

She takes out a piece of paper and opens her phone book and writes down a phone number. "Her name is Lingh. Call her. Call her right now!"

"I will! I'll go outside and call. THANK YOU! Affordable housing has been impossible to find, and I have all but given up."

"Don't give up," she says, "You can live here."

I feel like I just hit the jackpot. I go outside and call Lingh and leave a voicemail.

This can be the answer to my prayers. This would prevent me from having to ask my father for money every month to cover my bills if I was to stay in Connecticut which is what he wants.

This could tie me over until something big happens – like my positions in the market pan out or my movie sells back in Hollywood!

This can be the perfect temporary solution!

Angie gives me her phone number before we leave, and she makes me promise to follow up with her on everything.

I promise her I will.

The next morning Lingh calls me back and emails me an application.

Even though I'm packing up my car to get ready to leave for the silent retreat, I spend hours filling out the long, tedious application.

She needs all my information; bank statements, landlord information, social security letter, *everything*.

I have no other choice but to comply and so I do.

But it's a long, complicated process. I'm informed there is one apartment that's available on the top floor of the third building but it won't be available until the end of the month, which is three more weeks.

"That's perfect," I tell her, "as I'm heading out to a retreat for two weeks."

"Okay, we will run your application, and touch base with us when you get out. I'll let you know if I require anything further."

"Okay, thank you."

When I see my aunt, I tell her the good news. "Angie saved the day! Thank you, Auntie Jo! What a God shot that was!"

"Who's Angie?" she asks.

What?

"Angie! From yesterday. Remember?"

I watch as my Aunt's eyes glaze over.

She doesn't say anything. Then she asks, "Who?"

I look down at Meg who's at our feet, and I rub her head. "That's okay, my love bug is going to miss you a lot, isn't she?"

Meg jumps up and down.

After packing up and doing loads of laundry, and getting everything into the car, we head out to Massachusetts.

"Bye, Auntie Jo!" I say waving, as we drive off. "Thank you and I love you!"

Meg is riding shot gun beside me, about to experience her first, glorious two week silent retreat.

And when we get out, hopefully, we will have scored our own housing!

Twenty-Four

Chapter 24

W e have a nice drive up to Massachusetts. It's less than three hours away and it's an easy highway, and Meg enjoys sitting beside me and staring out the window.

She always has this look on her face like she's monitoring my driving. *"Careful, mom! Careful. Or you're swerving, you're swerving!"*

It makes me laugh.

I'm looking forward to this retreat, and I'm convinced that I will come out a different person, or the world will be different when I get out.

I'm so glad not to have to stare into an iPad for two long weeks and search for housing. I'm also glad not to look at the stock market and watch it running higher or check my emails to see the lack of response from Hollywood.

I'm glad to leave it all behind.

I have had it.

I'm burned out.

I need a reset. And this two week silent retreat will be that reset.

I have to find a store that sells stamps and then a mailbox before going in because "Lingh," my new supposed landlord, was becoming a real pain in the ass telling me she couldn't run my application until she received the forty dollar application fee.

I hardly have any bank checks left – I mean who uses those anymore anyhow, and so I told her I would be mailing cash and asked if that was okay.

It took forever to get a response out of her, and after making me redo my application three times because she said my writing was "too sloppy," my patience with her was running thin.

Also, she told me that the apartment Angie told me was available was taken by a man who requested a transfer, and he lived in an attic apartment and so I could take his.

An attic apartment?

She also explained it barely had windows. I was already getting a bad vibe but I was desperate.

She said the rent would be $917.00 a month and on my $2596 disability payments, it would work.

It has to work, I realize, as I pull over to a general store and purchase a stamp and an envelope to mail her the money.

I have had it with landlords at this point. All landlords.

I remind myself that my father ployed me with coming back east because he was purchasing a second "Florida home for the winters," and I could live there in that until he and my mom needed it, but of course that never happened.

But what bothered me more was that I needed to rely on my father for this to happen anyhow.

It was all so overwhelming, and I just wanted to mail this money off to Lingh, my new jail keeper, and head into this retreat, and forget everything.

When I find the meditation center thirty minutes later in a town in the center of Massachusetts, it's as beautiful as it looked on the internet.

The building is tall and made with brick and encompassed by four huge, white cement pillars.

What surprises me is that it's right on the street and being that we're in the middle of no where, I realize immediately, the place has no grounds.

There's a parking lot and a few buildings, but no large parks or greenery where my dog can run.

I unclip Meg from the car and we make our way inside. They were nice enough over the phone and made special accommodations for me and the service dog. "Hi," I say, entering the empty place and seeing one girl in the office. "I'm Juliana and I'm here for the retreat," I say, smiling. "I'm a little early. I'm here with my service dog."

"Oh, yes, yes, Juliana," a young, crunchy woman says, "We spoke on the phone, I'm Tina. Welcome!"

"Hi Tina, it's great to meet you. I appreciate all your help."

Meg stands beside me and Tina walks around to the dog. "What a cutie!"

"Yes, thanks."

"I know we're not supposed to pet the dog, because she's working, correct?"

"Correct," I nod, not wanting anyone to touch Meg anyhow.

"I'll show you to your room."

"Fantastic. Can you tell me, how many people are expected?" Like other retreats, I am assuming maybe fifteen, twenty tops.

"We have one hundred people registered," she replies.

"One hundred?!" I gasp. "Really?"

She nods.

That's a lot of people, I think as Meg and I follow her. "Wow."

She leads me upstairs to the second floor, and I am very pleased with the room.

It has two windows and it's on the end. It overlooks the woods and I can smell the blooming lilacs from the trees outside. There are communal showers and from there, I take the key she hands me and start to load my stuff inside.

This takes a long time because the parking lot is far away from the main building, and I have to bring everything like my own sheets, blankets, shampoo, clothes for two weeks, and all of Meg's food and treats and dishes and toys.

By the time this is done, I lie on the bed and turn off my phone while leaving my iPad buried in the trunk of my car.

Meg sits on the floor beside me and I feed her and once she's done eating, I envelop the silence.

Peace at last.

Twenty-Five

Chapter 25

~∞∞~

The problems at the silent retreat begin immediately. When I have to go to the bathroom, I am given the stark reminder that the rooms don't come equipped with bathrooms; you have to walk down the hallway to seek out the communal toilets. I find my room key, whisper in Meg's ear, "I'll be right back."

I make my way out of the room and descend down the empty hall.

I hear Meg squealing and jumping at the door of our room, and her long nails are like knives, frantically scratching at the door.

I turn around and go back for her, realizing that she's not going to stayed holed up in that room for one second without me.

We are both alike in two distinct ways: 1. We both can't stand confinement. When we were last at the vet in South

Carolina, she was cowering underneath the bench and one of the doctor's assistants bent down and tried to pull her out for the doctor and Meg would not have it. She growled. Low and loud. As if saying, "Do not mess with me."

"You better back off," I said in Meg's defense. "Give her a minute," I added and then tried to gently pull her out for the doctor. The second one is noise: She hates it. Any kind of noise, especially loud banging or shots or thunder. Forget it, she turns into a wet noodle and runs for cover.

Undeterred, I leash her up and take her into the small bathroom with me and close the door.

The space is tight. I am bent over trying to urinate without having to touch the public toilet seat and it's a disaster. I'm trying to wrestle Meg who is starting one of her panic attacks and going in circles. "Hang on, honey, hang on!" I whisper, as I flush the toilet and we make our way out of there.

Then, it's time for dinner. By the time we get downstairs, a line of people is already formed.

Everybody is staring straight ahead and there's a rope dividing the hoards of people waiting for the buffet table. From what I can gather it is merely shreds of lettuce and various vegetables, and the soup, from what I can smell, is vegetable with no meat.

I'm starving by this point and will eat anything. I am hoping the soup is good and the bread that it's served with is warm of which I will load on the butter, if they even have butter, and I don't really like or use butter anyway but I need sustenance.

This traveling and lack of funds has whittled my body down to 100 pounds and I am 5 4". Meg is even thinner. We need to bulk up.

Fast.

As we stand in the line, I can feel the angst. The room is not filled with locals; I can tell that immediately; many have come from all over the world, many from Asia. They're coughing and sniffling and I try to have compassion.

At other retreats, on the first night, we were served a nice meal and all got to speak to one another before it turned "silent."

Not here.

Here it starts now, and you can cut the animosity with a knife.

Meg is pulling on her leash while we stand in the line and she's sniffing the back of people's legs and it's utterly embarrassing and I can't even apologize because there's no talking.

I can't tell her to heel so I tug on her leash hoping she stands close to me but she's now close to sixty pounds and this is not an easy feat

Plus, you think people would give me space with the dog.

No. They won't.

They need to inch as forward to the food as THEY POSSIBLY CAN, EVEN IF THEY CRUSH ME AND MY DOG IN THE PROCESS.

The massive clock on the wall clicks to 6:00 p.m. and a GONG goes off.

Two people on either side of the line unhook the rope and people grab their dishes and make their way for the food.

Now lots of clanking can be heard; plates, spoons, forks, clattering and I watch as people stare at the plain vegetables taking lots of time deciding which ones they want to put on their plates as if they are choosing which person they're going to marry.

Chapter 25

"Let's GOOOOO," I WANT to scream, but I stand there as Meg keeps pulling on her leash and now she has it in her mouth.

I am trying to juggle a tray, the food, the hot soup, and the bread and Meg, who is pulling me.

Nobody comes to help and I can feel the awkward stares. Meg lunges forward and the tray nearly goes flying but I manage to hold it all together and sit down at the "reserved" table they put me at in the corner where I can sit with the dog.

Of course nobody comes to sit with me so I'm there alone receiving mean looks by the other participants due to the fact that I lugged a German Shepherd along with me to this silent retreat.

At least she's not barking! I think to myself, as I eat some of the hot soup and pick at the salad.

Meg won't sit still AT ALL, so I just give up, hoping she adjusts to this retreat somehow, and with half of the food left on the tray, we make our way out of the cafeteria.

She's relieved to be outside, and quite frankly so am I, and we walk around the grounds and learn there is no place to go or walk other than back and forth to the parking lot. The grass is not cut and I'm wondering why the place isn't kept up better landscaping wise.

When we get back up to the room, I want to brush my teeth before the 8:00 pm first meditation practice kickoff, but the faucet doesn't work. There's no water coming out of the small sink in my room.

I rush downstairs with Meg to tell them, and they send someone up who fixes it.

As I'm thanking him, I see something black on the rim of the baseball cap I'm wearing. I take it off and I look at it, and

123

say, "Oh, there's a bug on my baseball cap."

He takes a look at it, and says, "Yep, that's a tick."

"A tick!?!!" I gasp. "Oh, my God! How did it get there?!"

"They're everywhere," he replies.

"What do you mean?!" I ask.

I stare at him holding my breath. I remember the horror story of one of the Beverly Hills housewives on TV having Lyme disease which is caused from ticks. I think my mother had it too, but since she never tells me anything about her life, I'm not really sure.

"Here," he says, taking my baseball cap. "You just flick it down the drain and run the water."

I nod. I'm aghast. This is disgusting. I'm wondering how many are on Meg.

I reply, "Well, I better get going, the meditation is about to start."

"Sure thing," he says, "Enjoy."

Meg and I get downstairs and we enter the massive meditation room

There's a hundred people staring straight ahead at us and now we're late, although it has not started yet.

Tina, the facilitator, gave me a seat way in the back corner where I can sit peacefully with the dog, and as I walk through with this massive German Shepherd, all I hear is gasps, and I can see all the dirty looks.

Was this a bad idea?

Maybe I'm imaging this?

Meg and I find our pillows and sit down, and I pull out the Benebone that I had brought for her and she sits down beside me and starts to chew on it.

The room is dead quiet and every bite she takes on the

bone, it slams down hard to the wood floor and with her paws wrapped around it, every time she moves her head to chew it, her tags jingle on her collar and she's making TONS OF NOISE.

She can't sit still and people are turning around to stare at us.

I'm wondering when this will begin, and other people are coughing and I can't see anything because I'm so far in the back.

Meg rises and starts pulling on the leash again, and I am determined to hear the opening remarks so I just ignore her.

A lady enters the room and starts giving some speech. I can hardly focus but I'm surprised at her tone; she is yelling.

She is making these long, grand statements emphasizing certain words for effect and she sounds ridiculous. "I KNOW. Many of YOU. Have COME. From all over the WORLD. And you are HERE. For ANSWERS. Answers to that great question of LIFE. And you are SEARCHING! SEARCHING FOR MEANING!…"

She hardly sounds serene or peaceful.

I know my meditation teacher that I've had since Covid, I just feel relaxed the instant she starts speaking.

Here, I feel I need to be on guard. The people here are like MEDITATORS on steroids.

These people are NO JOKE.

I thought that coming from LA and having gone to so many meditation sessions and doing so much yoga, I'd have the leg up.But not here. This is next level.

Meg and I give up and go back up to the room. Apparently, word got around that she was causing a ruckus, and one of the facilitators knocks on my door and hands me a headset.

She informs me that I can listen "to all of the sessions from my room going forward."

Fine.

I'll just stay up here alone with the dog, like a dog, I think.

I was hoping for some nice community, maybe even make a few friends here, but I can tell right away that's not going to happen. So again, it's just me isolated with the dog.

Meg looks up at me from the floor.

I look back at her.

She retrieves her green ball and brings it to me, looking up at me with those big brown eyes. "Oh, my darling," I whisper. "Tomorrow will be a better day."

I throw her ball and she fetches it, excited I want to play.

I throw it again, repeating, "It will be better, my love."

But will it?

I put the headset on over my head after wiping it down with soap and water and listen to the woman who's still ranting.

"We all want peace and harmony but how do we get it? How HOW? HOW?!"

I hope some kind of answer surfaces.

But none does.

Twenty-Six

Chapter 26

T he next forty-eight hours at the retreat center are murder.

I wanted so much to like the place. I was so excited for this adventure of finally being on my own again with the dog and having my own space for two whole weeks.

It's not that I didn't enjoy my aunt at the convent, but it was a lot getting woken up every morning, and then finding things to do daily, and things to eat.

I was looking forward to the peace here and the meals that would be provided.

But it's all impossible.

Starting with sleep.

The walls are paper thin. You can hear every cough, sneeze, whimper, and breath.

The person across the hall from me had decided to bring some high speed mechanical fan and it's so loud, you can't think. It's obnoxiously loud. It resonates into my room and down the hall.

On the second night, I knock on her door at 2:00 a.m. "What is that NOISE coming from your room?!" I shriek when she opens it.

"Oh, my fan? Is it bothering you?"

THIS IS A SILENT RETREAT! SHUT THE FUCKING THING OFF, I WANT TO SCREAM! WHY THE LOUD NOISE THAT'S DISTURBING EVERYBODY?!

We are all jammed in these little, tiny rooms right on top of each other.

And Meg is bored. She keeps playing with her ball and it sounds so LOUD every time it smashes to the cheap wood floor.

On no sleep, I decide to be the first down to breakfast which begins daily at 7:00 a.m.

I arrive at 6:55 a.m. and many have the same idea because by 6:57 a.m. the line is already out the door. I get a plate of oatmeal and this time I'm smart enough to bring a large shoulder bag so I can take whatever items I want with me, like fruit and muffins.

It will be easier than to have to juggle that tray with Meg pulling me in different directions.

But more problems are to be had at the coffee station. As in, they don't serve it.

That's right, NO COFFEE.

Luckily, I brought tiny packets of decaf with me that I will mix them with hot water. You have to bring your own mug, which I would have done anyway, and I'm excited to have my coffee.

The problem is, with my arthritis, I cannot open the packets!

Frustrated, trying to pick these things open, I can't do it. I can't ask anybody because there's no talking.

Annoyed, I walk all the way down to the car with the dog, ditching the oatmeal to grab a scissors.

I put it in my bag, and go back to the coffee machine to start over. Successful now with my coffee, I realize they don't have SUGAR.

I down the coffee and soon realize that sitting in the meditation room with the dog is futile.

She will sit for maybe four minutes top before causing a ruckus in the room. It's not worth it. So we sit up in our private room together and stare out the window.

It's like being in a prison.

The withdrawal from life in doing this comes on hard and strong. No sugar. No internet. No stock market. No emails. No news. I can't bear it. It's like coming off of drugs.

I'm so used to being so jacked up on the adrenaline that all this brings me that I feel like I am dying.

I keep leaving the room with Meg.

We walk around and it helps a lot. Until we return to the room and we are flooded with ticks.

They are everywhere. On the inside of my pink jacket, on Meg, and even on the walls and in my bed.

I blow a GASKET. I MEAN REALLY BLOW A GASKET. I go DOWNSTAIRS TO the station where there is "help," if you need it.

Yeah, I need help. BAD.

"What's up with all the ticks?" I ask, curtly. "They're everywhere! I feel that being that I was bringing my service dog, I should have been notified of this!"

"Oh yeah, the ticks. Annoying, aren't they?"

"Annoying?! They're everywhere! Why don't you guys cut the grass?! How is my dog supposed to go to the bathroom?"

As if they care one iota.

The next time I venture outdoors with the dog, I am buttoned up head to toe in a baseball cap, a hoodie, and a scarf and look like I'm wearing a hazmat suit.

We give up on the food because other than the fresh fruit, it's inedible. The hoards of people here are ill, and the constant coughing and sniffling is unbearable.

Everywhere you go, you have to use your hands to open door after door, touching door handle after door handle, so I wear gloves.

It's GERMS GALORE.

I am determined to tough it out though!

It's only for two weeks, I think. And plus, I have NO PLACE TO GO!

I have no HOME TO GO BACK TO!

If I did, I would have already left. Actually, if I did, I wouldn't have joined up to begin with.

I've done silent retreats before. For me, it's a one and done. You do it, check it off the bucket list, and try something else.

Two days in, I find a note on the bulletin board with my name on it.

This is for emergencies like if your family is trying to get a hold of you or something like that.

I reach for the note and it reads, "Hi Juliana, this is Todd, the retreat manager, I'd like to speak to you. Can you come to my office immediately?"

Yeah, I IMMEDIATELY get a bad feeling.

Something is up. *What could he want to talk to me about?*

I enter his office with Meg, and the poor thing is looking so lost and baffled, wondering, What is the PURPOSE OF ALL OF THIS, MOM?! WHY WHY WHY!??!

Todd comes out, nods to the dog, and says, "Let's take THIS outside."

I nod, and Meg leads us out the front door.

We walk down the driveway and he's not saying anything, so I start, "Oh, Todd, it is so beautiful here."

"Really, Juliana, is that what you think? Because I wanted to check in. How are you DOING?"

I had to say the right things. I was trapped.

If he kicks me out, my new apartment isn't ready for another month, and I have no place to go. In New England, the hotel prices are sky high.

"Things are great, Todd! I'm so glad I came. There are so many people! Wow! I didn't think this was going to be so popular."

"Oh, yeah," he stutters, "we really pack them in. They come from all. Over. The. World. Umm, you see, Juliana, we've had some complaints. The dog, you know..."

"Oh, yes, she's no trouble. She's such a great service dog..."

"Yes, but we're having some people complaining. The ball, when you're playing with it in the room, it's disturbing the people underneath you, and we've had many, many complaints."

"Oh, the ball... Gee, I'm so sorry. Yeah, I get it. We will stop immediately."

"Well, actually, what we we're thinking is... we want to move you out to the other building."

"The other building?" I ask.

It took me HOURS to load all of my stuff into our room, and I liked our room. It had two windows and it was on the corner. And I can smell the lilac trees outside.

"Yes, we want to move you right away due to all the complaints we're having."

"Ummm hmmmm," I say, appeasing him. "Sure, no problem. Happy to," and I grin.

When I get back to the room, there are more ticks. *And I mean they're everywhere.*

I can't stand it.

I find a huge blister on Meg's nose and wonder if she's been bitten.

I call my childhood friend Katherine, who lives only two hours from here in New Hampshire.

I'm now in a panic. "I think Meg was bitten by a tick, Kat! I need to take her to the vet right away!"

"Come up here, and I'll get you an appointment."

I think about it.

Moving to another room is not going to solve our problem. Meg needs help. And she needs it now.

They are adamant they want me out of the main building with the other participants, and by this point, I have had enough.

I inform them that I am leaving, and I want a full refund. I'm going to need the money for the road.

I begin unloading my room which is a huge chore going up and down the stairs.

The girl who is supposed to be watching Meg in the car, is going through my stuff in my car when I come out, and I am shocked. "What are you doing?" I quip.

"Oh, I'm just helping you put the things in the car."

I get a bad feeling. My gut tells me she's lying.

"Please don't do that. Just stand here and watch the dog. I

need to pack the car a certain way so everything fits."

She nods, and I stare at her.

I see she's carrying a bag. I remember reading the information before coming and how one of the rules was "No stealing." I thought what a strange rule to have. Who would come to a silent retreat TO STEAL?

I need to get Meg to the vet and don't have time for this.

I hurry up, get everything into the car, and we're off.

"Sorry, sweetheart," I say to Meg as we drive out of there, a measly forty-eight hours later.

I turn on the radio and blast it. "That was a disaster."

A few days later when I'm cold, and I'm looking for my investment banking fleece vest that was lying in the back seat of my car, it's gone.

The bitch stole it.

Karma.

Twenty-Seven

Chapter 27

❧

D riving up to New Hampshire is fine, but I'm not ready yet. I'm not ready to be back out in the real world.

I'm excited to see Katherine who I haven't seen in twenty-five years, but I'm also embarrassed that I had to leave the two week silent retreat so early.

And what would my parents say? *Oh, we KNEW that dog wouldn't behave! We knew Juliana couldn't hack it!*

I would need an excuse, something good, but other than the ticks and Meg's poor behavior, I would have stayed.

Wouldn't I have?

Where was I going to sleep tonight, I wondered, as I drove down another endless highway with Meg beside me in the car.

With everything on an "app," and phones being useless, you couldn't even call a hotel to book a room. I had to deal with about ten different "hotel websites," to score a decent hotel rate.

And room service – that was long gone, which means I'd have to hunt down more food; more time standing in a restaurant to-go line and paying sky high prices. I longed for the days of nice, five star hotels, when stays were enjoyable.

I enter New Hampshire and find the town where Katherine lives. It's nice, another small town, not too much unlike the suburban, quiet town in Connecticut we grew up in.

I need to go to the bathroom, walk and get exercise for Meg, and lock in a roof over our head for tonight.

Katherine has three animals; a big dog and two cats, and with her financial predicament being worse than mine, I would not put her out in any way by attempting to crash at her place. She has her own problems, not to mention her health issues..

I pull into a restaurant parking lot so I can go to the bathroom; but they're not open yet. I am already five minutes late to meet Katherine and I need to put on some makeup and clean myself up somehow.

I do this in the car, still having to go to the bathroom, and when I arrive to her apartment complex a few minutes later, she's standing outside waiting for me.

I wave to her from the car window and I am as giddy as a little kid.

I park in the first spot I see and cross the parking lot. She looks the exact same; maybe gained a little weight, and her hair is a lot shorter. And grayer.

She has since turned into a lesbian over the years and mentioned that I was her first and only "true love." Another reason why I won't spend the night there. But I push all that aside. "Katherine," I say, enwrapping her in a big hug. "How are you?! Thank you for getting us the vet appointment."

"Sure…"

Meg is still in the car, and I say, "Let me introduce you to Meg!"

I open the door, unclip Meg and she jumps out.

Katherine pets the dog, and she's not afraid of her the way most people are of German Shepherds. "Awww, she is so cute!"

"Thanks!" I reply. "This is nice," I tell her, looking around.

She lives in a peaceful apartment complex that's surrounded by a lot of trees and nature.

"Yeah, I hate it! The neighbors are awful and my apartment is in the BASEMENT! Come on, I'll show you!"

I nod and follow her to her little dungeon that yes, is in the basement and right across from the noisy laundry room.

Nothing has changed with Katherine, her apartment is just as sloppy as her house was when we lived next store to each other as kids. I giggle as I walk around and pet her animals. It's like old times.

Our houses were opposite, mine was a large contemporary that my father designed that rested on top of a cliff; and hers was down the road in a smaller ranch barn style house. She had horses, too, which was cool. She was always an animal lover.

I still need to urinate and I don't want to impose, so when we go outside to take the dogs to the park, I see a swimming pool and ask her if there's a bathroom there and gratefully, there is, and I tell her I'll be right back.

I bring Meg and I go. Relief at last.

Once you are on the other side of fifty, finding places to go to the bathroom while on the road is brutal. Makes me not like being on the road at all. Plus, with my arthritis, sitting for long periods and not knowing when I can lie down again is hard.

At this, I wonder how long it will take me to get settled with housing. I just want to be "home."

When I get back to the dog park, Katherine reminds me that our vet appointment is in thirty minutes and tells me to follow her over since we shouldn't ride in one car with both dogs.

I do and as we drive, I am looking around for hotels. I see a Marriott which looks rather decent and I'm trying to figure out what road I'm on so I can remember to stop there after the vet. It'll be much easier than trying to find something on my phone while being parked on the side of a road somewhere.

We go into the vet, and the exam goes by quickly. I don't know how the doctor figured it out, but she tells me there are no ticks on Meg.

She says as long as I've kept her up with her Simpatico Trio, she should be "fine."

She also says the scab on her nose is not a tick bite. She explores the advantages of giving Meg the Lyme disease vaccination with me, but I decline.

After Covid, I am anti-vax, and though I wondered if I should inject her, my intuition says otherwise.

I tell her I'll think about it and thank everyone profusely.

After paying for the vet appointment, I tell Katherine that I need a shower and that I'll call her later and take her out to dinner.

When I find the hotel right after the vet, there's rooms available and being that it's a Tuesday night, it's under $200 a night, so I check in with the dog, and I'm so grateful for a hot shower and my own NON-COMMUNAL TOILET.

They have a restaurant down in the lobby and I order a well done cheeseburger and fries and run down to pick it up as soon as they open.

I stop at the hotel store on the way out and buy peanut M&Ms for dessert and get a Diet Pepsi.

Score!

I devour it with Meg with the TV on, watching the nightly news, with my iPad in my hands and I'm in my glory.

I text Katherine that I'm spent and I'll take her out tomorrow night, and I'm asleep by 8:00 p.m. in the queen size bed that I couldn't be more grateful for, with Meg safely in the other bed beside me.

Twenty-Eight

Chapter 28

When I turn on my phone the next morning, I go through all the texts I received while I was in the retreat center for a whopping three whole days.

I click through them while in bed, with Meg still sleeping in the other bed beside me.

The poor thing didn't sleep last night because there was thunder and lightning and she didn't have her cage to run into, so she hunkered down in the wet shower.

I felt so bad for her.

I had to go in there and get on my hands and knees and console her, and I can't wait to get my own place and all my belongings back, including her big cage...

I let Meg rest, and I keep clicking through the texts of rando guy after rando guy.

One guy I met in Vero Beach writes, "Question... Are you a woman who is uncomfortable when a man shows interest in you... Asking for a friend," and it ends with a smile emoji. Another writes: Hey, I'm thinking about you. Others from across the country ask: Where are you?

I never respond to the "The W's." *Where are you? Who are you with? Why aren't you with me. When are you coming back?*

So many guys, all over the place, and I could care less about them the second I'm gone.

I don't know why.

I don't know why nothing ever clicks. Maybe because my own mother never loved me, deep down I don't think any man ever could either.

Maybe I just couldn't stand the entrapment; the watching them eat, breathe, clean themselves, go to the bathroom.

The only person I could ever remotely think about that with was Noel. Not only was he really smart – and I don't mean just book smart, but he could read any person and any situation exactly like it was and we always saw it the same way. And plus, he was clean. Pure.

There was a purity to Noel that other guys just didn't have. Maybe it was his spirit.

So as I sit here, deleting text after text, I wonder, with hotel living being so dismal, why not now just move in with somebody? They're all are homeowners...

But just the idea of it.

The idea of seeing somebody first thing in the morning and then the last thing before I went to bed...I couldn't imagine anything worse.

I had a similar conversation like this with my best friend in LA, Ezekiel. He's an attorney and always living a solo life in different apartments like me, dealing with landlords... And he said to me recently, "You know, I thought about having a sugar momma, but then I thought, nahhh..."

I laughed out loud! "Oh, me too! Just the idea of it, Zeke! I'd rather live on the side of the road in a ditch!"

It's funny to have a friend who understands you this way. Most don't. Most couple up, merge, ride the wave together.

I'd rather be alone.

Freedom is bliss. And you can't put a price tag on it.

I delete most of the texts and remember that just up the street, over the bridge, is Maine.

I call out to Meg, "Let's go sweetheart! Time to have fun!"

Twenty-Nine

Chapter 29

It's an easy drive up to Maine, and once we get off the bridge, right down the street is a Dunkin' Donuts.

I enter the drive-through and order two donuts; one jelly and a vanilla crème, an orange juice, a nice cold water, and a medium coffee with skim milk, sugar and a straw, and we head towards the almighty ocean.

Bearing right off of the main road and heading East, I sip my delicious hot coffee and munch on the donuts while holding the wheel, and up ahead I see it before me — the beautiful, powerful, majestic Atlantic ocean in all of its splendor.

I park on a side street, and get out of my car. The wind offers a chilly caress, and it's soothing, comforting.

I let Meg out, "Look how beautiful, darling! The ocean!"

We stand at the edge of a cliff, and the sea before us is vast, powerful, and beyond human comprehension.

The waves roughly lap the shore, saying "hello," every few

seconds. It's a reminder to enjoy every single moment, because we never know when the last one may be.

As we walk closer, we find a park and go in. The park runs over the cliffs, and there's lots of people jogging and admiring the view.

It looks like a magical oil painting with the oceanside homes tucked into the cliffs, and there's a natural sacredness to it all. It reminds me of Malibu.

All of my problems just wash away as I breathe in the fresh air and get exercise.

There's a bench along the walking path, and we sit down and take it all in.

I snap some photos of Meg with the beautiful ocean behind her.

I feel, for the first time, this was where I was meant to arrive. That right here at this place, in this moment, all seems right with the world.

I feel so close to the workings of the natural world, like I'm taking part in or witnessing something holy.

The pictures of Meg come out great and I post one to my stock social media account, writing, "On top of the world!"

Yes, I may be homeless. *Right now.* And broke. And my dreams went up in smoke.

But I'm free.

And there's always the new hope of tomorrow.

I drive around with Meg later to look for hotels in the area, and I'm thinking to just park it here for a few weeks and relax.

But we quickly learn that the hotels here are not only expensive, they're all booked up since Memorial Day weekend is coming up.

That grave feeling washes over me again as I start to get

hungry and need to use the bathroom.

Meg is getting tired and it's a long drive back to the hotel in New Hampshire.

I get prices as I stand in another run down motel lobby, and then I ask if I can use the bathroom while dragging Meg inside with me.

I can't even afford the cheap hotel, and I wouldn't want to stay here anyways, so I go outside and call my father.

"Oh, hi Dad!" I say when he answers the phone.

He's supposed to think I'm still deep in the silent retreat and unavailable for two long weeks, but he doesn't seem surprised at all when I call.

"What's going on?" he asks.

"Dad, I'm in Maine! It's beautiful here! I just went to visit Katherine!"

"What happened to the retreat?"

"Uh, yeah, Dad, it didn't work out." My voice drops as I say it.

I really wanted it to work. I could have used two weeks of nothing after being kicked out of the South Carolina apartment, and learning this new relationship with Meg.

"Okay," he says, not even bothering to ask why.

"It was the ticks, Dad!" I tell him, "They were everywhere! Meg was full of them! We had to leave."

"I see, so now what?"

His question hangs in the air.

I have no fucking idea, Dad. Every hotel I check into costs a fortune and I can hardly afford anything close to you and Mom, but then I remember, Lingh, and the affordable housing.

It feels like a long shot, but it's all I have to hang on to.

"Dad, I can try to find an apartment up here," I say, "but

wouldn't it be too far away from you and Mom?"

He doesn't say out loud what I know to be true, that my mother doesn't want me anywhere near her so he throws his money at the situation.

Always.

"Look, Julie, whatever you want, I am here. Stay up there, get a lobster roll, enjoy yourself. Find a nice hotel. I'll pay for it. Then if you can't find something you like up there and you want to come to Connecticut, I'll help you pay the rent."

I flop down on a stone wall outside of the hotel and watch the cars go by.

Meg is on her leash beside me, and I feel relieved that my father says this, but also like a burden.

This was not my plan to leave LA and come to the East coast and be a leech on my father.

This whole thing bothers me immensely after I had fought hard for jobs and cheap rent in LA to make it as a writer there, and the whole thing was supposed to pay off.

I wanted to sell my screenplay, make a good living, and be a working writer. That was THE PLAN. But like plans often do, they implode.

I feel like a failure.

"I don't know, Dad. I mean I appreciate it, but the hotels here are so expensive, and even if I do find a place to live here, I'll be four hours from you and mom."

"Don't worry about anything," he says. "Just stay up there until you figure it out."

I would have rather he said, "Just come home, stay here with your mother and I for a while," but that will never happen.

So I'm trapped out here on the road and my father will just pay for it all.

145

My father brings up getting the lobster roll again and it sounds great, but they are like forty dollars. "Just enjoy yourself," he keeps saying. "Take Katherine out for a nice dinner tonight."

"Okay, Dad. Thanks."

I hang up and call Lingh.

I know I can't live here in Maine, and I know I can't afford Connecticut on my own, and this Lingh is my only shot at being close to my father, but not depending on him for money.

I leave her another message, "Umm, hi Lingh, it's Juliana, I just wanted to check in and see how my application was coming along. I ended up leaving the retreat early and I think you said the unit would be available in June, but I can move in sooner if that's possible. Please get back to me, thank you."

I hang up and it all seems futile.

Meg takes a dump and she looks relieved, and I feel anything but.

I pat her head, "Good girl, darling," and I take a crap bag out of my purse and pick it up and I look around for a trash can to dispose it.

We get in the car and we're off again.

To where?

Who knows.

Wherever the wind takes us.

Thirty

Chapter 30

I head back towards the beach in Maine; only this time I drive further north and I come across some condos by the ocean that say "weekly rentals."

I dial the phone number as I walk Meg around the area and leave a message.

I want to find a beach so I can sit down and relax but I see nothing, just tall cliffs and ocean. There's restaurants that are situated along the side of road which rest upon cliffs.

There has to be a beach somewhere I think, and I get back in my car, start driving again, and call Katherine.

"Hey Katherine," I say into her voicemail, "Umm, I checked out of the Marriott; it was too expensive and I'm over here now just over the bridge in Maine. My dad says he'll pay for a hotel while I look around here for housing and if you want to meet me and go to the beach and get a lobster dinner later, that will be great!"

My line is ringing and I click over and they're calling me back on the condo I just called about.

They tell me it's $1,000 a week. That seems reasonable, I think, and it will buy me a week's time but then they tell me it's a two week minimum.

I ask if I can see the units first, and they tell me yes, and they will call me back with a code.

I drive back over there and wait.

It's already 1:00 p.m., and the clock is ticking.

While I wait, I walk around and get rates for other hotels, and they're either sold out or $300 plus a night.

My phone finally rings and I'm told there's four units available and they ask, "You don't have any animals, right?"

"Umm, I have a service dog."

"You have a DOG?!" they clamor.

"Yes. But legally, they have to –

I am cut off.

"Legally nothing. These are private units. Owned by private owners. They can rent to whomever they want. They don't want anybody who has a dog," and they hang up.

I'm shocked.

Katherine calls and she's in some kind of fit, acting as if she's just got possessed by the devil, and I'm trying to understand what's wrong with her. "This WEATHER!" she screams, "There is NO WAY I'm going to the BEACH! IT'S TOO FUCKING HOT TOO FUCKING HOT JULES, I CAN'T TAKE IT TOO HOT TOO HOT!! I CAN'T TAKE IT!!"

It's not that hot and I can't deal with her now because Meg is pulling on the leash, and I'm walking aimlessly around the area getting tired.

Katherine can't stand the heat and I can't stand the cold, and

I can only imagine what the winters would be like if I stayed here in Maine, and I decide this whole thing is not going to work.

I get back in my car and we leave the state.

Connecticut is only three hours away and if I stay in a lousy town called Danbury where my Dad used to have his business and he lives in the next town over, it has to be cheaper than here because it's not a tourist destination.

Meg and I drive on highways that seem endless, and I call a hotel I'm familiar with and I don't get a good feeling from the guy on the phone, but I make a reservation anyhow, giving him my credit card, and when I arrive four hours later, I'm told that they're sold out and they don't have any record of my reservation.

I am frustrated by this point.

As in *really frustrated.*

When I take Meg out to the back of the hotel where I finally see some greenery so she can go to the bathroom, some guy comes out of no where, and says, "That's not allowed!"

I'm in no mood to argue, I let Meg do her business and go across the street to another random hotel which is owned by a friend of my father's who he sold his business to.

Next door to it is a Stop & Shop and that was built on the land my father had his company on; a big cement block factory. I used to work there with him when I was a young girl.

I drop my father's friend's name to the hotel clerk who seems totally clueless and they give me a rate of $149.00.

The lobby elevators aren't working, the place is completely empty and eerie, and they inform me I have to use the service elevator around back to get up to the 7th floor.

I use the hotel cart to lug all my stuff up; my clothes, pillows, blankets, plants that will die if leave them in the car which I have been dragging around with me since I left LA, and all of Meg's food, dishes, and toys.

When I get to the room, it is the most disgusting room I have ever been in in my life.

The rug is old and raggedy looking; the paint is chipping off the walls, the shower doesn't look like it's been refurbished, let alone clean for twenty years, and it smells like asbestos and mold combined. In a word, it is horrible.

Too tired to argue or get a better room, I need to take Meg out again to go to the bathroom and decide I'll get a sandwich at the deli next door at Stop and Shop for dinner.

Back into the service elevator we go which looks like it's not even safe, and we go into Stop and Shop and I don't really like taking Meg with me into food stores but I have no choice.

The deli looks as dirty as the hotel and I just purchase some crackers, a yogurt, nuts, water and an apple, and head out the door, thirty dollars later.

I need a plan.

Why couldn't I have a mother who says, "Oh you're in town?! Come over! Stay as long as you want!"

My grandmothers always welcomed me. Always took me in. And this whole experience is a stark reminder that they are long gone.

I want to cry, and I go back up into the room and try to sleep, but I can't. I look out the window onto the highway outside and I can't believe my father's company is no longer there and it's now a Stop and Shop and so much has changed yet a lot is still the same.

I never liked Connecticut; it never felt like home to me, and now I am here with no way out.

I am running out of money; or should I say available credit on my credit cards, and I need to find sustainable housing soon where I can park it for a year or two to decide my next and hopefully FINAL MOVE in life.

Meg is on her own bed, and she looks comfortable and cozy, and I go to her to give her a belly rub. She just ate and she seems fine. "I love you, poo poo," I tell her. "I'm going to figure this out for us, my love."

She licks my hand.

"Don't worry, I've got you," I say, giving her a little smile. And I rub her belly some more. "Is it playtime? Do you want to play with your ball?"

She jumps up and grabs her green ball on the floor and brings it to me, wagging her tail.

And right now, all that matters, is that we play, have fun, and we stay in love.

Thirty-One

Chapter 31

I wake up the next morning in agony, both physical and mental; I'm not sleeping well and I'm worried about the future.

I check Meg's nose, it's looking a little better, but this room smells, the windows don't open, and I have to get out of here.

My body is uber sore from the arthritis and the constant lugging of our belongings from place to place and getting pulled on the leash by Meg. And I'm sick and tired of digging into a plastic bag for my underwear.

I turn on my phone in search of a better hotel. I quickly find a Marriott close by, call the number, and miraculously a live person picks up the phone.

"Hi, I'd like to check in this morning. What are your rates? I'll be staying about a week."

They give me a decent weekly rate and I give them my information, pack up our things, and head right over. The hotel in the same town, Danbury, but closer to the town line of where I grew up, and it's a world of difference.

There's greenery, it's far off of the highway, and when we enter the lobby, the sweet smell of a hot breakfast with eggs and waffles wafts through the air.

I check in and I have a beautiful room that overlooks a mountainside! It is peaceful and immaculate. It has a desk and two queen size beds; one for me and one for Meg, and a huge TV with WIFI.

I'm in heaven.

I take a HOT shower in the marble shower, and then I rush downstairs to get breakfast before they close while leaving Meg in the room.

I need to eat and I can't afford to get the stares from the people while in the buffet line if I bring the dog.

I load my plate with fluffy, hot scrambled eggs and a waffle and I bring a bag and grab dry packets of cereal and some oranges and two cups of hot coffee with TONS OF SUGAR.

I get back to the room with it and I share it with Meg. *Hot food! What a score!*

I haven't eaten real food in days.

I turn on the TV and watch the news. The market is still running higher and I am still short, holding onto a volatility product that has decay. My mood sours again when I realize I need to make that money back to get out of this hole.

I console myself by reminding myself that I'm not paying rent anywhere or utility bills. Still the hotel and food bills are out of control. I need to get settled and fast.

My father comes to visit me the next morning, and I'm so happy to see him. We have breakfast outside together, he looks great, and he loves Meg.

Meg jumps all over him and it's unreal how German Shepherds can just walk all over you if they think they're the alpha male in any situation. My Dad is intimated by her and Meg picks up on this and milks it for all it's worth.

She sits by him and grabs at his plate of eggs with her paws, and she doesn't relent until my father gives up and feeds her his entire plate.

I am so tired and worn out at this point, I cannot fight any of it. I just let the dog do whatever she wants and laugh when she makes me laugh which is all the time.

I explain to my father that I'm looking around for apartments in the area, which means I'm making good use of the hotel stay, and it is not a total wash.

However, there's barely anything available and when my father comes back two days later to see a one bedroom with me that's in a nice area, the place inside isn't great, and it's $2600 a month.

I am not paying that! I cannot afford that on my disability payments.

I do not want to be in a position where I am expecting money from my father every month.

After a full week of looking, Meg and I move towns and hit the Connecticut shoreline, Branford, more specifically, to find housing.

Plus, it's closer to the affordable housing option that I have with Lingh.

We check into a Holiday Inn which is nice and the room is big but for a Holiday Inn, it's also expensive.

The summer is here and this is a more touristy destination since it's on the shoreline. Due to the high amount of spring weddings, there's barely an available room here, or even at other hotels in the area for that matter.

The clock is ticking and I just want to get settled.

Lingh finally calls on the affordable housing and says, "It'll be just another week until the unit is available," however she reminds me again that, "The tenant who lives up in the attic moved into the one bedroom where Angie lives so once we clean up his attic apartment, then that will be available for you."

She also mentions there is only one small window.

Great.

I'm not liking any of this at all.

She still hasn't finished processing my application yet, and I feel that she is completely useless.

And how can I live in an attic apartment?!

I hire a realtor and continue my search for housing.

I want to give up, I want to throw in the towel, I wish I never left California, but I have made my choices, and perhaps they were bad choices, but things were never worse when I left Santa Monica, and I was not safe there anymore, and I did what I had to do.

It will all work out in the end, I tell myself.

Won't it?

Meg is on my lap as I peruse apartments on my iPad. She gives me a little kiss reminding me that we are on the right path.

Thirty-Two

Chapter 32

❧⟳❧

M y uncle fixes me up with an eighty-five year old real estate broker, and though she's nice and looks beautiful for her age, she's more trouble than she's worth.

Often times she sets up appointments only for me to get there and she's no where to be found. She'll call later and tell me that she was lost, and when she finally arrives, I'm waiting outside, annoyed and tired with the dog, and the place is just a disaster. The units I'm shown are old, need work, and smell like mold.

We look at both things for sale and for rent because my father is still adamant that he can buy me something although I know with the overpriced valuations this will never come to fruition.

These escapades exhaust me, and then there's all the back and forth with my father, "Well, did you like it?! What are you going to do?! Huh? Now what?!"

The hotel bills are racking up and I have no idea how I'm going to pay for it all, and when the weekend comes, the rates at the Holiday Inn get ratcheted up to $350.00 a night.

$350 A NIGHT FOR A HOLIDAY INN!!!!!

I move hotels again, and I find one far away from the Connecticut shoreline in a town called Wallingford, and I book two weeks there at the Marriott.

It's on the side of a highway, but the place inside is absolutely beautiful.

It has a restaurant in the lobby and the room they give me is on the ground floor on the inside of the building which means I don't FACE the highway and get this – it has a sliding glass door that opens and a little balcony with a tiny tree outside.

It's heaven.

It really is.

It is frequented by mostly businessmen, and it's by far the nicest room I have been given on this trip from hell. The shower is marble and immaculate with spotless glass doors. The room has central air and the AC works great.

It is incredible the difference your state of mind and being is when you're living in a nice place.

All the other hotel rooms barely had windows that even opened a crack, if at all, and all that stale air was killing me.

Here I'd leave the sliding glass door wide open while running the AC if need be.

It was fresh air galore. *Oh, the small pleasures!*

I realize, after all this, I should just be a writer for HOTEL REVIEWS! Lord knows I am living in them all!

From here, I give up on the real estate agent and hunker down with Meg.

We attempt to get into a normal routine as if this is our home.

In the mornings, I walk Meg around the hotel so she can go to the bathroom, and then on our way in, I get a cup of Starbucks coffee, and a plain box of cereal with no milk.

If I'm feeling wild or desperate, I go for the latte, but at $8.00 a pop, this is a rarity.

Then if I'm not doing laundry in the hotel machines, we go back into the room, and I straighten things out and have CNBC on while watching the market from the balcony and sipping my coffee. The mornings are heavenly, and I can hear the highway traffic outside and I'm grateful I have no job to rush off to.

After a nice hot shower, I lie back down on the bed, and search for housing until 1:00 p.m. Usually, I find nothing.

Then, Meg and I venture out on our "gang walk," wearing our matching bandanas, around the highway and the side roads.

It's not bad.

There's a little farm up the road and sometimes we walk there and look at all the plants. They're expensive, and I don't have a home yet to bring them back to anyhow.

When we get back to the room, it's time to watch the market close, and then figure out food. I usually order take out every other night because the hotel food is inedible, and then I save half in the room frig for the next night.

I eventually order a hot plate online so I can make my own hot tea and instant coffee so I won't have to keep spending so much money on the overpriced Starbucks in the lobby. This is money well spent.

I keep pestering Lingh as to when the attic unit will become available so I won't have to bother my father for money, and she never responds.

She is the most useless person on the planet.

I end up getting a call from her a week later and she tells me that the "roof is leaking," and now it will be months until the "attic apartment with no windows," becomes available.

Oh, great.

I want to scream.

Great, Lingh, thank you, you useless DUMB F%:+'df piece of %#$e/.

I am livid.

But I'm trapped and can't take my frustration out on her.

She is my wild card.

She is my only hope at this time.

Gone are any relatives or friends or family who will take me in. Funny how that happens.

Then, one day, Lingh calls out of no where, and she tells me that there's a unit available two towns over from Branford, and there is a glimmer of hope.

But when she gives me the street name, and I immediately pull it up on my iPad, I see that it's right near the highway.

I tell her it won't work, but ask for the address anyway. Meg is on her period now and she has been bleeding all over the sheets and it is probably only a matter of time until we get kicked out of here so I am getting more desperate by the minute.

That Sunday, I decide to drive over there with Meg.

Worst case, there's a beach close by, so if it is terrible, I can just take her there and we can still enjoy the day.

And when I pull up to the address Sunday morning, some-thing short of miraculous happens.

159

It is not an apartment complex. The address turns out to be a little house! And it's on a dead end street! It is half a house and the house is shared with one other tenant and it has only one shared wall! *There's no one on top of me or below me!*

I think I'm dreaming.

When I get out of the car and walk around, it's actually adorable.

Meg and I survey the premises. The other houses are bigger and look a little run down, but all in all, it is not bad.

The place is locked up, but I walk onto the balcony – yes it has a little veranda, and I peak inside the window.

It's messy inside with the stove pulled out, and it has an old refrigerator, but it doesn't look *THAT BAD!*

"Poopie, what do you think?!" I ask Meg. "Is this our new home?!"

She keeps sniffing around.

I am amazed. I don't know what the rent would be but I email Lingh immediately and tell her that I have decided to take it and ask her when it will be available.

I walk around to the back of the house and I see that the neighbor has their door open. "Hiiii," I say. "My name is Juliana!"

A guy surfaces, and he's a decent looking guy around my age. We start talking and the first thing I ask him is if there is any crime here. After all I went through in LA, I am still suffering from PTSD.

He says no, never, and says he has a learning disorder and that's why he lives here.

He seems nice enough and no red flags go off.

I cannot BELIEVE IT.

HAS MY SHIP COME IN?!

I drive off feeling happy and grateful, and hope that I can land this. I'm relieved that I never blew a gasket with Lingh over my earlier frustration, and hope she can close this for me in a timely manner.

But who knows.

Her track record blows.

But if it does work out, I won't have to rely on my father, and I'd be close by. I cross my fingers and say a prayer.

I drive over to Dunkin Donuts to celebrate because it's time for a treat, and I get some hot coffee and donuts, and I take them over to the beach with Meg.

It's still early in the morning and there's not a lot of people around and I let her run free on the beach and she goes swimming in the water. She's having a ball, and I love watching her.

I sit in the sand and inhale the ocean air.

The beach is adorable and so close to where I would be living.

I can't believe it.

Maybe lady luck is turning the ship around!

Thirty-Three

Chapter 33

This girl Lingh has to be the biggest idiot on earth. We agreed I would take the unit, but I wait three more weeks in the hotel at $150.00 *PER NIGHT* for her and the damn maintenance team to get it together. She's dragging her feet.

It's surreal.

I'm so sick and tired of giving Meg water from the hotel bathroom sink which takes ten minutes to fill because the water comes out so slow like molasses. And I'm running out of clean underwear.

I'm sick of the highway and the fumes and the noise.

On the weekends, the parties at the hotel are unbearable. People talk in the hallways at all hours of the night; slamming doors, laughing, yelling.

It's their right; hell, they're on some sort of vacation. But not me, I am *living* in the hotel.

And I can't wait to get out of it.

I do everything I can not to lose my temper with Lingh. They will not rent to somebody who's a loose canon, and I keep telling myself this.

The only reason why I hang in there is because A. I have no other options. B. I'm not renting another shithole at $2500 a month where I have to ask my father for money every month and

C. There's security in affordable housing. Like rent control in Santa Monica, the landlord can only evict you if you don't pay the rent. And thanks to my monthly disability payments, that'll never happen.

And unlike the rogue landlord in Florida who was the property owner, they can't make up erroneous lies and take me to court. And unlike the corporate conglomerate in South Carolina who has an army of attorneys at their disposal, they can't just "decide not to renew my lease."

No, this is solid.

This will lock me in for a while. It's surreal to think of all that I have been through.

Housing should never be this hard. I'm quiet, clean, and have steady income. I don't have parties or do other bad things.

Throwing somebody out of their home who is disabled and has a service dog should be illegal.

And living on the road trying to find a new one – IN OUR CURRENT HOUSING CRISIS – is impossible, and something I wouldn't wish on my worst enemy.

If I didn't have any available credit left on my credit cards, I literally would be living in my car. And the car is twenty-six years old.

I'm somebody who did everything right my whole life; I

attended grad school, worked hard for the past forty years, always had good jobs, only to get rug pulled again and again and again.

It was a dog eat dog world. And I'm hemorrhaging from it now.

The last straw comes when I wake up in bed with Meg since the hotel room only has one king size bed and not two queens, and her paw goes right into my eye.

She pokes my eye out and I never screamed louder before in my life.

Over and over again, I scream out in pain.

I'm sure the entire hotel hears me, and I worry I'll never be able to see again.

I think I'm done for.

Without my sight, I can't read and I can't write, and it's the only thing I love to do. Besides looking at the ocean and nature.

A friend of mine who I rarely speak to happens to call, and when I tell her what happened, she says something I will never forget. She says, "Juliana, perhaps this is the universe sending you a signal. And when you are able to see again, you will start to look at everything differently."

I will never forget those words.

She's right. The truth is, I'm still bitter from my mother not taking me in, I'm bitter that my once very close sister abandoned me during this time of need, and I'm bitter for my father who condoned all this bullshit and never, with all of his money, bought "that second condo home," he promised in Florida.

He said the timing wasn't right and I trust his business sense, but this was not the original plan.

Chapter 33

And I hated Connecticut.

But I was doing what everybody else did, which was to go home to be close to their elderly parents. *But how do I manage this when my mother won't even speak to me on the phone?*

My father keeps saying she'll come around... but *will she?*

Lorna calls and I tell her what happened. She tells me to get to a doctor immediately. "What doctor, Lorna?! I don't have healthcare insurance!"

"You're disabled," she responds, "What do you mean? What about Medicare?"

"Our trusty system has the disabled wait two years for Medicare!"

"Well, you better get healthcare immediately. You do need it, you know."

"And what do I use for an address, Lorna?! The hotel?!" I'm beyond upset and I can't take any more drab conversations. I hang up, "Lorna, love you, just pray for me, okay?"

Miraculously, within twenty-four hours, my eye heals.

I don't know how and I don't know why. Maybe it was all my prayers.

Maybe it was karma for rescuing the dog.

Dog spelled backwards is God.

I have a God, and God sees all, and I believe God heals all.

That dog really got me good, and I can't explain it; I can only thank my lucky stars. But this, like everything else, will be left behind, and I will just keep moving forward...

When Lingh calls the following week, she finally has a move in date.

We're meeting on Thursday, June 27th to sign the lease.

I'll get the keys.

And a new home will be mine.

Thirty-Four

Chapter 34

I spend the next forty-eight hours at the hotel ordering a new bed and new furniture for my new home.

I find some wicker chairs with soft cushions on sale at Macy's and I purchase the same bed I always get every ten years which is a Sealy Posturepedic for $800.

Things are really starting to turn around.

The only problem I run into is that it takes almost a week for my bed to arrive and I'll have to spend the first few nights sleeping on the floor.

I thought about staying longer in the hotel, but no thanks.

When I wake up Thursday morning, I tell Meg our journey is coming to an end.

"Darling, we're getting the keys today to our new home!" I coo with excitement, and I give her an extra squeeze before we sail out the door.

When we arrive at 1:30 pm to the new house, the workers

are still busy putting in the new stove so we don't go inside because I don't want to get in their way.

I have to get a dog license for Meg so we head into town and visit the Town Hall. Everything is easy breezy, the people are nice, and I don't even have to pay a licensing fee because Meg is my service dog.

As I drive back to the new house, I'm nervous. I have never been inside of it, so I have no idea what the vibe or smell is.

I am meeting Lingh at 4:30, and I figure, for the price, whatever the problems are, if any, can be fixed.

I'd rather pay $917 and deal with a more corporate landlord, than pay $2600 in rent and deal with an actual homeowner to fix any problems. Corporate has bigger pockets. And they have to follow protocol. *Usually.*

Also being that this is some sort of "government housing," they can't just jack up the rent every year to sky high prices so I feel like I'm already winning.

Aren't I?

And when I get there early, I enter the unit.

And there's a smell. *A really bad smell.*

What. The. Hell. Is. *That?*

The overweight workers are taking their time installing the stove and there's wreckage of their work all over the place.

I look around and the place is no where near ready. I try not to interrupt them but I need to ask if they can hammer in my new cable rod so Meg can stay outside on the chain.

They seem annoyed at having to do this for me, but once Meg is fine sitting outside in our new front yard, I begin to unload my car which is filled to the brim.

The workers don't speak English so I can't ask them about the odd smell. It's like an odor of toxic cleaning chemicals, and underneath that, mold.

Like really, musty, *toxic mold.*

The place is absolutely filthy.

There's a tiny wall AC unit that they're running at full speed which hardly puts a dent into the blasphemous heat in the place, and I open up all the windows for some sort of cross ventilation but there's no breeze.

I can barely breathe inside, and I need to go outside.

I tell myself that once I keep all the windows open over the next twenty-four hours, it will air the place out, and when I come back there will be no smell.

Right?

I hope so. I still have one night left at the hotel.

The workers finish up their work, and when I question why the odd things are still outstanding like the house has never been power washed as promised, the front light is still hanging out of it's socket, and the screen door doesn't lock, they just shrug their shoulders, and say, "No English."

Sure.

No English.

They understand exactly what I'm saying.

But I figure I'll just deal with it all with Lingh when she gets here.

They leave and there's no love lost there, and Lingh arrives late with her assistant, they're both put out that they have to sit on the floor with their slew of documents that I need to sign.

We all hunker down on the dirty floor, and the process takes over an hour, and I just want it to end. Meg is getting antsy and I want them out so I can start cleaning this place.

Top to bottom.

Maybe I'll get it fumigated.

Who knows.

We do a walk through, and there's a massive rust spot on the shower floor and when I mention it to Lingh, she responds with, "I'll see what I can do."

Same with all the rotted wood in the floor, the broken window, and the massive hole in the ground in the front yard where there seems to be some sort of wild animal living.

The problems seem insurmountable, and I feel overwhelmed.

I have never moved into a place as disgusting as this.

By the time they leave, I'm exhausted and can't do anything further, and I hope they fix the things they agreed to fix.

Although, somehow, I highly doubt this will happen.

Call it a "gut feeling."

Either way, I've had enough for today.

When we get back to the spotless Marriott hotel, I nearly kiss the ground I walk on. It smells great and it's spotlessly clean.

I'm anxious to peel off my filthy clothes and get into that marble, shiny beautiful shower. I want to wash the grime away that I'm covered in and the stench that permeates my hair.

Is the place really that bad?

Is it really that fucking filthy?

Yes.

Yes, it is.

Thirty-Five

Chapter 35

"**D**o you smell something weird?" I ask my cousin, Emma, when she comes over.

She's three years older than me, and we've always been close but I've always lived far away, and now that I'm in Connecticut, I'm glad she'll be in my life again.

I've been helping her with her father who has dementia for the past two weeks while I was staying at the hotel.

"No, I don't smell anything weird," she says.

We're sitting on the new wicker chairs.

The new bed still hasn't arrived, so I've been sleeping on the floor. Also I was woken up out of a sound sleep when the "workmen" never replaced the fire alarm batteries in God knows how long, and both fire alarms began chirping.

It was not how I wanted to start off *at all*.

Luckily, Angie, the ninety-five year old friend of my Aunt Jo, sent over her handyman friend, "Frank," who helped with

170

these problems. He also assembled the furniture and installed a new toilet seat.

I look over at my cousin, and she looks as exhausted as I am. She's a principle at a elementary school for disabled children and she's also managing taking care of her parents. Her mom and mine are sisters.

"Emma, I don't know how you do it. I'm here to help now in any way I can. I know my journey in finding housing wasn't easy, but I landed, and now I'm here for family."

I look over, and she nods.

She's sipping from a lone bottle of water I had in my refrigerator because I hadn't gone shopping yet.

Meg is sitting on the floor between us taking everything in.

The windows are open and I'm still airing the place out.

I think I *will always* be airing this place out.

I watch my cousin, and can't help but wonder why she never invited me to stay over at her big house in Hartford, Ct. Even during the weekends, when the hotel rates rocketed to over $300 a night in Connecticut, never did she ask, hey do you need any help finding something? Would you like to spend the night?

Maybe it was the dog, I tell myself.

Yet I remind myself that I dropped everything to go over to take care of her father when she needed me, when every second mattered to secure housing for me and Meg.

Whatever.

It's water under the bridge now. Like everything else.

"Em, are you okay?" I ask.

"Yeah, yeah, I'm fine."

"Okay, good. Look, I know you've been through a lot. You're doing too much. With work and your parents and your long hours and commute, it's a lot."

My cousin outright owns her house and she has money so she could retire, I just couldn't understand why she didn't or wouldn't.

"It's okay, Ju, I'm used to it."

"Retire!" I tell her.

"Yeah, maybe."

Some people are addicted to their routine. It's a lot for some people to just sit with themselves without their incredible schedules.

"Come on, show me your new place," she says, rising from the wicker chair.

"Okay," I reply, and I walk her around my small, humble abode. "This is the big closet," I tell her, opening an empty closet door. "My room is there, it's so quiet and faces the woods, and here's the bathroom. But look at that rust spot," I say, pointing to the shower floor.

"Oh, just get a bath mat and cover it."

"Really?"

"Yeah."

"It's kinda gross, isn't it?"

"But you won't see it with the shower mat."

I look at her and I guess that's just this family's way. *Just cover it all up.* The place may be on fire, but as long as you don't look at THE FIRE, YOU WON'T SEE IT!

My cousin is on my mother's side which is where most, or should I say *all,* of the dysfunction resides. My father's family is as perfect as a family could get.

So I guess maybe I'm only half insane.

Who knows.

I drive my cousin over to the Lobster Shack later and I really enjoy her company, and we sit outside and eat two lobster rolls while looking at the water of the Long Island sound.

It's tranquil and pretty. Meg is at my feet, playing with her Benebone and watching the seagulls.

My cousin insists on paying, and she tells me it's to thank me for helping her with her dad.

I thank her. "Awwww, I appreciate that. Thank you, and no worries," I say, "Anytime, that's what I'm here for."

We drive home, and I feel good. I love my cousin, and I'm so happy I have somebody in my corner here in Connecticut.

We hug goodbye and make plans to see each other soon. "Goat yoga!" I tell her. "In Madison!"

"Sounds great!" she agrees.

If you bet me a million dollars that I'd never see my cousin after this, I'd say, sure, I'll take that bet.

Well, I'd lose.

I would be out the million dollars, because my cousin ghosts me after this, and I never hear from her again.

But that's not the worst of it.

When my stuff finally arrives from South Carolina and Frank, the handyman returns with a friend to help me unload everything out of the tiny port-o-potty cube, and they set up my TV and leave, the cable man arrives.

He tells me he needs to access "the crawl space," to reach the cable lines.

"What's a crawl space?" I ask.

"It's like a small basement, let's go around back."

I follow him around the house and in the back, there's a tiny wooden door.

It's about twelve inches high and it's closed with a wooden peg.

"It's in there?" I question, confused.

He nods.

He removes the peg, opens the door, and crawls inside.

And then he turns around, and walks back out with an absolute look of horror on his handsome face.

"What?!" I gasp. "What is it?"

Thirty-Six

Chapter 36

I watch with my mouth gaped open as the cable man crawls back into the crawl space and starts whipping out trash bag after trash bag, and other junk, and it stinks to high hell.

Horrified, I call maintenance.

Just as I'm about to leave a voicemail, two maintenance guys magically appear. They come barreling down to the crawl space area, and I turn around and say, "I was just calling you! Why is this area under the house filled with mounds of heaping garbage?!"

They shrug.

No English.

"I don't get it, wasn't this cleaned out?!"

The cable man comes out and he's covered in dirt and grime and can't breathe.

"This is NOT his job to be cleaning that!"

"Hey, man," the cable guy says, as cool as a cat, "I just need to reach the cable lines." He shakes himself off, "But I can't with whatever is in there."

I'm stunned.

Didn't the prior tenant have cable?!

Why is there such a mess down there?

I rush back upstairs to get paper towels for the cable guy so he can wipe off his face and hands. I douse them with water and orange disinfectant soap that I keep at the kitchen sink and I bring them back out to him.

He grabs them from me like I'm handing him a life jacket, "Thanks."

The two maintenance men go in there and start lugging furniture, unused crates, and other bags filled with trash or who knows what, and they just leave it outside right under my bedroom window.

They say, "We'll send a truck for it tomorrow," and they take off.

"What the HELL?" I say, staring at the cable guy. "Well, can you access the cable lines NOW?"

Three hours with the cable guy and we still can't get a signal.

The truck never comes to take away the trash as promised, *surprise, surprise*, and it rains all over the garbage. The entire area under my bedroom window stays soggy and gross for weeks, and the cable man, who now has my personal cell number, unlike my cousin, keeps calling me nonstop.

He says, "I'm anxious to return to get the cable going for you."

Yeah, I'm anxious to get the cable going too.

Meanwhile, I have no internet and no TV and feel completely isolated in this small town in Connecticut with no

176

access to the real world.

The first few days it's nice, but now I'm getting desperate.

I wait for the cable man ALL DAY to come on a Friday, and he calls me at 6:00 p.m., tells me he's lost, and asks for my address AGAIN.

I give it to him and wait.

He calls me an hour later, and asks, "What town do you live in again?"

"What *town*?! What do you mean?!"

I give him the town and he tells me he's at my address but in a different town. He says he's *only* forty minutes away. He assures me that he's on his way, and to wait.

I do and regret every second of it.

He arrives at 8:00 pm, and tells me "He's off the clock," and "Doing this for me as a *favor*," since he knows that I "Want the cable so bad."

He *is smoking hot*.

But I don't care.

I want MY CABLE AND MY INTERNET!

The days longing for "hot guys," are long gone. Just fix me up with some WIFI! Sad but these are our times. And this guy is shit out of his luck.

He tells me that he can't hook up the cable now, and he has to go home because it requires a "specialized agent."

Yeah, sure.

Get out, go!

Days and hours are spent on the phone with the cable company, and they finally send someone over who knows what they're doing and the hour finally arrives, *Houston, we have contact!*

There's the signal on my TV and I make sure I have CNBC

so I can watch the market and I'm set.

While this new cable guy is setting everything up, I'm on the phone with Walmart haggling over a price issue, and when the cable man asks me what he wants my WIFI password to be, I just blurt out Walmart, but he spells it wrong, so now it's Walmark.

Goodbye everyone, just get out of my life and my house and when I shower later and put on some clean pajamas ready to curl up with my dog and some hot chocolate in front of my huge TV, I can't help but notice all the trash that is still underneath my windows in the bedroom, and so I close the blinds, pretending it's not there.

And pretending that this has not been my life.

This place is a total shithole.

But at least I am not living IN A HOTEL shithole, I remind myself.

I get on the couch, Meg is already there waiting, and I give her a little squeeze and zone out to the brain fog of the internet and boob tube.

Thirty-Seven

Chapter 37

O ver the next few weeks, I do everything I can to get settled. I have loads of laundry to do and though the house didn't come equipped with laundry machines, they had hookups so the first thing I did was go right into town to the local hardware store and bought my own BRAND, NEW MACHINES.

IT'S A DREAM COME TRUE.

They arrive the next day, and I am in laundry heaven.

I do load after load, washing everything from my clothes, to my jackets, and all my blankets and sheets and towels. I buy high end laundry detergent and fabric softener and my whole house smells like fresh, clean laundry, and my clothes are perfectly clean.

I can't even describe how happy this makes me.

I know I'm paying for water and gas to heat the water, but I indulge and it's worth every penny.

My home is still piled high with unpacked boxes and I go through them one by one.

Everything that needs to be cleaned, gets thrown into the large laundry room. It doesn't have shelves and it's jammed with the water/gas energy tank, but it's fine.

Every day, I clean and clean; scrubbing the floors, the windows, the door handles, and I even take apart the kitchen and bathroom sinks so I can clean the pipes, and the grime and gunk that comes out is horrendous.

I find old food in the cabinets; macaroni and cheese dated back five years, old microwave popcorn packets, and other gross items and I throw it all away, while using gloves on my hands.

In a few days, things start to look up.

It's still warm outside, and I keep all the windows open day and night. Meg gets to sit outside and enjoy her sun baths, and I always have one eye on CNBC.

I'm sleeping great since my bedroom faces the forest and things are blissful.

Meg and I start taking long walks in the neighborhood, and though there's a main road that neither of us likes, once we get into a private condo community that's up the street, it is much easier for us to walk. It is hilly and picturesque and there's so much nature and wild animals to observe.

I end up meeting a nice girl who has a dog and she's a little older than me. Her dog is on the dumb side and it's named Tumeric. It doesn't mesh well with Meg but the woman is okay; she's a nurse and her name is Marla.

We exchange phone numbers and start to do stuff together like go to state parks, and we bring our dogs. She's sort of boring, but it's good to get out, though our dogs never hit it

180

off.

One night, we go up the street to a ho-down where there's music and dancing. She doesn't want to bring the dogs, and it's a mistake. It's outdoors and Meg would have enjoyed it.

I sit and watch everybody get drunk, including Marla, and it's one of the rare nights I go out and leave Meg home alone.

I decide I won't be doing that again; I have more fun with Meg, than without her.

The next week, I get an email from an old mentor in Los Angeles who's a professor at UCLA and she informs me that she's going to be in upstate New York for a retreat.

It's in October, and the leaves at that time will be spectacular. I decide to go and I register, and I'm excited to see her in a few months.

As the days pass by, as much as I want to feel at home in this new place, every morning I'm waking up with sore throats and headaches.

I'm not sure why, but I feel like I have been run over by a train. I'm sleeping great because it's so quiet, but I feel "off."

One random morning, I go around to the backyard to investigate the red shed, and I find it.

That smell!

The dank odor I cannot get rid of that's been seeping into this house.

I put my nose near the small crawl space screen window, and *there it is!* That *stench!*

Now I know where it's coming from!

When Angie calls me later that afternoon, I run it all by her. "I don't understand it, I feel sick all the time. I can't figure out what that smell is. Every time I contact the landlord, they tell me they will send somebody over. And when they come, they

181

tell me, "It's all in my head."

"Of course they do! Call the health department!" Angie yells into the phone. "Have them look at it!"

"Really?"

"Yes, that's their job! Get it checked out!"

"Okay, you're right, Angie, thank you."

I click off and I call. They say they will send somebody out within days.

To cover my bases, I even call my own "Mold company," for a free estimate. *What could possibly go wrong?*

Plus, it's free.

So when the mold company comes over, and they go in to inspect the crawlspace, they come out more horrified than the cable guy.

As if that's even possible.

"Yeah, I've never seen have anything worse," the guy tells me when he crawls out. "There's black mold all over. You're going to need a Hazmat team in there. You've got everything in there; trash, mold, dead animal carcasses…"

I hold my hand up to stop him. I'm getting nauseous. "Please, don't tell me anymore. I can't —"

He moves his camera in front of my face, "Well you better look at these photos. You said you're a renter? You better call your landlord asap."

I call Lingh, who by now thinks I'm a royal pain in the ass, like every other landlord I have ever had, and I can't believe I am having these kind of problems or conversations.

I have waited so long to move in here, and at this point, I'm just crumbling.

Mold man keeps telling me to look at the photos.

I can't. "Thanks for taking the pictures," I tell him, "but can

182

you just email them to the landlord?"

I give him the email address and he sends them, and before I know it, Meg and I are displaced, and living back at the hotel again.

Thirty-Eight

Chapter 38

It's been three days at the hotel and the landlord hasn't even started on the work.

I get the crackpot Lingh on the phone. "Lingh, I don't understand it! I have been saying since day one that there was mold in that house, and now I'm right. Your maintenance workers told me it was fine over and over again! Now I'm displaced with my dog!"

I wait for her response, nothing. "Did you see the photos the professionals took?" I ask.

"Yes," she mutters. "We saw them."

"How quickly can we get this remediated?"

"Ohhh, well," she stammers, "I'm going to have to run this by corporate for approval..."

"I am sick, Lingh, living there. It needs to get FIXED!"

"I'll get back to you," she says.

When the health department arrives for the inspection, it is even worse than anybody originally thought.

And now that they're involved, the landlord finally starts to take action.

They promise me that I'll be out of the hotel before the weekend, and the hazmat team goes in and begins the job. But I learn that when they're half way through finishing the project, they have to stop mid-way because the landlord reneged on the funding.

There's plenty of back and forth on who's going to pay for what, and money and payments, and they finally come to an agreement and the hazmat team finishes their work.

But after the crawl space gets cleaned out, the landlord is now refusing to pay the mold remediators to complete the project. I think the whole thing is costing them twenty grand.

Back at the hotel, Meg and I couldn't score our original old hotel room, and our room is different this time. Even though it's still on the ground floor and it faces the inside courtyard, it doesn't have that little tree outside of front our balcony, and it's a totally different vibe.

Staring up at the ceiling, feeling like there's no end in sight to this madness, I do something I haven't done since I got Meg, and I start crying.

Long, drawn out, heavy sobs, and before I know it, there she is, jumping on the bed, and licking my face, with her paws on my chest.

Pinning me down, her eyes say, "Don't cry, Mom. We got this. You're doing a great job."

But I feel like a failure. Failure in securing safe housing for this dog and I. *Something that should be so easy.*

And of course, my family is no where to be found in my time of need.

Thirty-Nine

Chapter 39

Autumn arrives, the leaves on the trees are starting to turn, and Meg and I marvel at the endless miles of brilliant colors. There is nothing else like fall on the East coast.

The weather is cool and crisp and the leaves are fluttering across the roads like confetti.

We try to make the best of hotel living again. We continue on our walks around the hotel, load up on the hotel store snacks, and visit the farm that's about a half a mile down the road.

They have all kinds of festive things; pumpkins, plump apples, cider, pretty plants, flowers, and it's uplifting and fun every time we go.

Of course, like everything else, it's expensive, but I purchase three miniature pumpkins at $1.50 each and I bring them back to my room.

They jazz up our room nicely.

The cold weather is rolling in, and I remembered to bring my own blankets, and Meg and I try to cozy up in the hotel bed.

Watching the news at night, there's war, famine, corruption, and I'm grateful I'm safe and secure in this little hotel room.

Though it's all going on my credit card, the landlord says they will offset my rent for the next few months and I take solace in that. Yet I don't really know whether to believe them or not.

They continue to drag their feet on the whole remediation process, and I'm wondering if I should hire an attorney.

Yet I have no money, *and who would take my case anyhow in this wealthy state of Connecticut?*

I can't call HUD because it's not Section 8, it is some private tax income credit housing, and I feel hopeless.

But as long as Meg is happy and safe and can play with her ball and eat her food, then we will live to survive another day.

The only person who calls to check on us is Angie, the ninety-five year old friend of my dementia aunt, and I'm careful how much I tell her because she feels bad for "Getting me into this."

I assure her that it's going to be okay, and that all of rental housing is this bad, and there's nothing I can do, but wait it out.

She gives me the private phone number of the housing CEO, and he calls me back after I leave a message, and his voice is like butter. He makes promises that he's "Handling everything," and says, "The worst thing I deal with is seeing our tenants displaced," and he tells me that he will call me "right back."

Another whole week goes by and I never hear from the guy.

I just surrender to the whole experience and start embracing the hotel lifestyle.

Every morning, I enter the marble lobby and hit Starbucks and by now, they all know me by name. I order a delicious, expensive grande vanilla latte extra hot, extra foam, and they make it perfectly.

I also get a hot cup of coffee to go along with it and a boxed cereal like Apple Jax. Some days, I even go full throttle and order the orange juice, and I save half in my tiny hotel refrigerator.

The little frig at the Marriott is actually silent and doesn't blare noise like the other hotel refrigerators and it doesn't keep me up at night. *Oh, the small pleasures!*

I tip them generously, because, well, *why not,* and then Meg and I sit outside on our veranda.

I lean my head back in the chair, letting the sun hit my face, and listen to the outside noise of the highway. I'm again grateful that I'm not one of those cars on the highway, miserable, and racing to work.

I sip my delicious coffee, and wait for the stock market to open.

I have a load of laundry going in the machines, and though it's hard with Meg because she doesn't like the small enclosed space of the laundry room, she runs Zoomies in the hotel hallway while I take care of business.

Luckily, we're far back in a desolate part of the hotel so nobody sees this huge German Shepherd barreling down the halls, doing spins and turns, looking like she's on cocaine.

I encourage her to have fun, and I keep telling her that, "We're on a wonderful vacation."

I get a call out of the blue from the landlord that a "Construction company is coming in two hours and to please be there at the house to let them in so they can examine any leaks," and they also have someone from a mold company, "Doing a test."

"Great!" I say, "I'll be there."

I rush to leave and when I get there, nobody is outside waiting for me, and the place inside still smells disgusting.

It's cold inside and the musty odor hits me like a ton of bricks.

I had to leave the windows closed in case of rain, and it's horrendous.

I leave the dog outside so she doesn't have to endure it and suffer, and a woman pulls into my driveway with an old beat up pick up truck behind her.

She gets out of her car, introduces herself, and she has a strong Russian accent. I don't like her from second one, but whatever, *what choice do I have?*

She walks around, looks completely useless, and instructs the dark skinned man to go around to the crawl space for the inspection.

Seconds later, another mold man arrives for the testing.

The Russian lady and the other guy take off, and as the mold man does his testing, he tells me that he has "been here before."

"Really?" I ask him. "Why?" Not sure I want to know.

"Oh, the other tenant here was mentally ill. He was a hoarder, and there were always problems here."

Great.

That explains it.

Everybody leaves and I'm back in the hotel with nothing accomplished.

I put on my clean pajamas and curl up with the dog, making sure I order the most delicious take out food I can find. I get a grilled chicken salad and a cheeseburger for Meg.

At this point, I am running up so much money on my credit cards, I really don't care.

I figure if I off myself, I'll never have to worry about all this debt, but then I think about poor Meg.

What would become of her?

She couldn't go back to Holly Hill and heaven forbid she ends up with my parents.

No, I wouldn't wish that on my worst enemy.

I decide to forget that I'm living in a hotel and lose myself in the evening news, and when the food comes, I tip very generously, while saving the receipt for the "expenses," and then Meg and I gorge ourselves and we're in food heaven.

We fall asleep soon after, tired and satiated, and I try to remember, that life could be always be much, much worse.

Forty

Chapter 40

The tall, dark skinned young man stares at me through his Hazmat suit, I hand him a cold Coke-Cola because I don't have any water. He throws the bottle in his truck.

"So you're going to be done in five hours?" I ask him again. We're standing in my driveway and I can't believe we are going through this.

His large lips are open and the one tooth in the center of his mouth sticks out like a sore thumb.

He nods.

"I really appreciate this," I tell him again, stunned that I have to deal with this on my own. The landlord, who should be here managing this project from top to bottom, is no where to be found.

Should I even be surprised?

I take a deep breath, and I can't help but feel sorry for this

191

man. He'll be underneath this house and in that crawl space for hours fumigating it with toxic fumes to kill off all the deadly mold.

All the money in the world couldn't pay me to do that job.

I am grateful to him, but I also feel bad. I think it's an insurmountable task and it's never going to get done, or never get done right, and this nightmare is never going to end.

But I take a leap of faith because I have no choice.

"Okay, I'll be back in five hours," I say. I get in my car and turn back, "Good luck."

Meg and I sit head to the beach, and we stay in the car and watch the water. I'm tired and drained.

The scenery is beautiful and I just take it all in. Meg seems tired, and the hours go by quickly.

When I get home, the guy is just coming out of the crawl space and he looks like he just returned from war.

"Are you okay?!" I ask, worried.

He doesn't move or say anything. "I'll go back inside and get you another Coke! Hang on!"

I go inside to get him another drink, as if this Coke is going to magically cure his experience of being down there in that toxic dungeon.

When I walk inside the house, the fumes of what he's done hit me in the face.

I cannot breathe. It is toxic with a capital T.

I grab the Coke and rush back out to him, "Here you go! How did it go?"

"I did you good," he says. "I did ya real good."

"Really?!" I ask. "Are you okay?"

"I took care of it for you, he replies, and he seems out of it.

"Thank you," I reply, "Thank you SO MUCH," and I send

him all the positive vibes that I can. If I had the money I'd buy him a round trip ticket to Aruba, or pay for him to take a cruise somewhere right now.

Nobody should have to do this job. Nobody! And I curse out the prior tenant who lived here before me and trashed this place!

"Hey, listen, it really smells bad in there. Are you sure it's okay to sleep here tonight?"

I know it's not. He doesn't have to tell me this.

But I already checked out of the Wallingford hotel and it's already been a long day, and it's getting dark.

"I've only done this kind of work on abandoned houses," he admits, "I don't know." He shrugs and gets back into his truck.

I call the landlord again, informing them that the house is still uninhabitable, and I'm going to another hotel.

I get their voicemail; nobody is there, they have all gone "home."

I throw WHATEVER I CAN into a bag and grab Meg's food and we head off again.

I'm furious. I don't even know where I'm going. I'm also starving.

Meg's looking at me like, *"Why, mom, whyyyyy? Why so many problems?"*

Suffering is meant to be endured and overcome. It leads to wisdom. And wisdom gained, is wisdom lived, which becomes wisdom shared.

"It's going to be okay, honey," I assure her, and give her a little squeeze. I turn on the radio, and Joe Cochran's voice comes blaring out of the speakers.

He's singing an old song that reminds me of LA, "With a Little Help From My Friends." Our artist group would have these holiday parties and Zeke used to sing this song in the choir.

I open the window for Meg and she sticks her head out the window and as the song plays, I sing along, loving the lyrics. I look at Meg, and she's now looking back at me with that look of love.

I turn back to the road. "Go back to the Branford Holiday Inn," a voice inside tells me, "just go there, it is close and easy."

I drive over there, a room is available, and they take us in. I'm too tired to eat, and I just fall asleep in a weird stupor.

The next day, the landlord calls.

They tell me won't pay for another hotel stay, and they instruct me to go back to the house "tonight."

I pack up again, and it seems to take forever. Meg waits patiently, and nobody will wait for you as patiently as a dog will.

We make our way back "home," and when we walk in, miraculously, it seems better.

I open all the windows, air the place out again, and decide to count my blessings.

Though I could stay home for a year without coming out, this weekend is that retreat in upstate New York that I already paid for months ago to see my old LA mentor. It's non-refundable, and I decide to go because it'll be worth it to see her.

I also have plans to meet my parents at a restaurant for lunch on Sunday on my way home.

I'm still tired and spinning, but who knows, maybe it'll actually be a great weekend.

Lord knows I could use one.

Forty-One

Chapter 41

❦

I dress in comfy jeans, and put on an LL Bean fleece vest with a pink Coach wool scarf over it. I carry a purse that's handmade with faux fur, and I head out for the weekend looking very "New England."

Though I'm still driving my twenty-five year old Mercedes, it'll be great to see my mentor and tell her that I got out of apartment living and I now live in a cute house by the water near my parents.

The scenery driving through upstate New York is beautiful. Meg and I observe the vibrant display of autumn colors, featuring brilliant oranges, yellows, and reds across mountainous regions and forests.

When upstate New York hits peak fall, there is nothing else like it in the world.

The peak foliage is jaw-dropping, and just to get to witness this makes it all worthwhile. The retreat center located in

Holmes, New York, which sits on over five hundred acres of forest and wetlands and hills of the Hudson Valley.

It's a rustic place, with a camp site that has a strong smell of burning wood.

When we arrive to the main location, there's nobody there to check us in. The bitter, dry cold air as we walk around on dead crunchy leaves keeps us on the move.

I was told that they made special arrangements for the dog and I but I quickly learn that all the rooms are "shared," with "bunk beds," and "eight girls to a room."

When I finally get to meet the "retreat coordinators," who are late, on first sight, I know we're going to have problems.

They're all Karens with a capital K, and they tell me, "I must share the room with the other girls."

I tell them, "That's impossible, I have a German Shepherd who has never shared a room with anybody."

They are of no help, my mentor is off to dinner somewhere, and I'm starting to wish I never came.

I've been driving all day, my arthritis is hurting, and I need to rest. I sit outside in my car and call my Lorna, who also knew my mentor, and she knows that we're close.

"She's always been a bitch," Lorna spews, "and now you can't find her? Did you call her?"

"Yeah, I called. She didn't even invite me to dinner. And now they're expecting me to sleep in bunk beds with the dog."

"Bunk beds?! How ghastly," Lorna replies. "Tell them they're in breach of the American Disabilities act and you're going to sue them."

I giggle. "This is not how I wanted this weekend to go. I was looking forward to a relaxing in the country with friends."

"Things never work out as planned," Lorna huffs. "Just go

home," she tells me. "Cut your losses."

"But I'm having lunch with my parents on Sunday. I'm looking forward to that."

"Then suck it up, but demand your own room!" she says.

"You're right. Okay, thanks."

After hours of arguing with these people, they finally take me to a private room but inform me it will cost an extra $200 a night. They tell me to Venmo them the money right now.

I can't even believe this. "Sure," I tell them. "No problem."

I reach for the key that's in their hands, and they don't hand it to me.

"Not until we receive payment!"

"Are you serious!?" I gasp. "I'm standing here with my service dog. It has been a long day of driving. Can I at least get my laptop in the car and unload some of my things first?!"

They look at each other confused, then nod.

I don't have a laptop in the car or any intention of paying them, and I'm wondering if Lorna was right, that I should have just left.

Instead, Meg and I stay cooped up in the $200 dilapidated room for the night.

The paint is chipping, the rug is filthy, and somebody's shoes have been left under the bed.

It's way too scary to walk around in the dark to try to find the meal room for dinner, so we go to bed starving, and when we wake up the next morning, I walk around to try to find my mentor to no avail.

Meg and I decide to take it all in stride. We enjoy the scenery and there's a lake, and I sit down on a bench avoiding the retreat sessions completely.

Meg begins doing the Zoomies, and most of the retreatants

look out at us from the big bay windows, and laugh.

I can see the people pointing as Meg has gone rogue.

I let her do her thing because I'm sure she's just as frustrated as I am.

She even runs *into* the lake, despite the "No swimming allowed," signs.

We tough it out for the rest of the weekend, being completely ignored by everybody; my mentor never responds to my texts, and Sunday morning, we drive out after forty-eight hours of hell and no food.

We get to the restaurant we're meeting my parents at early, and I'm starving and I remember that they have this great sausage and red onion pizza that I used to get "to go," when I was staying at the hotel in Danbury.

I can't wait to order it, when my parents arrive, for whatever reason, the hotel is completely empty and so is the restaurant.

We get a table outside.

Meg is on a leash tied to the table and she's walking around smelling the area.

I put my faux fur purse on a napkin to protect it from the dirty table, and we order, and my parents seem distant.

They hardly ask about my retreat, and when I tell them how disappointed I am that I never got to see my mentor, it goes in one ear and out the other.

"It just wasn't at all what I expected," I add.

My father says, "Did Meg eat? I don't want her grabbing at our food when it comes."

"I have some food in the car. Should I get it?"

"You better," my father replies.

"Okay. I'll go get it and I'll get her bowl. Watch her okay? I'll be right back."

I go to the car and come back with Meg's food, and during all this, the pizza had arrived, and my mother and father began eating without me. *No prayer, no nothing.*

Also, I see that the filthy napkin that my purse was sitting on, had been used to BLOT THE GREASE OFF THE PIZZA. "What did you do?" I splutter. "That napkin was dirty."

They are now eating the pizza doused with the filthy napkin and they don't even hear me.

I'm so hungry, I start to eat it and regret it the second I do, because it tastes off, like dirt.

It has been all that I have been looking forward to for the past two days and now I can't even eat it.

I debate ordering a new one, but the main course has arrived, and I'm starting to feel sick anyhow. I take a bite of the meat, and it oozes grease out into my mouth, and it doesn't even taste like meat.

There's no conversation at the table and I feel so disconnected.

An hour later, Meg and I are driving home. I pet her head, and say, "Sweetheart, that was a bad weekend, but it's over now. Okay? I love you."

She seems to agree with me, and more than anything or anyone, I feel one hundred percent connected to this dog.

I have come to love the dog more than man.

I can't wait to get back to our home, and get into our own little world again.

And unless it's a five star hotel, I am never leaving my house again.

Forty-Two

Chapter 42

Relieved to finally be home again, when I enter the house, the smell is still there. It's not as bad, but it's *there*.

Angie has connections all over town and gives me the name of her attorney, and I jump all over it. He gets involved as a favor to her and before I know it, I have an exterminator coming bi-weekly paid for by the landlord.

There's a woodchuck living under the house, and the exterminator handles it, and the landlord also installs a screen door in front of the main door so Meg doesn't get attacked by it.

It makes a world of difference.

Plus, the exterminator handles the crawl space issues, and puts out bait for any mice, and also cleans out dead animal carcasses.

It's time consuming and nasty, but it gets resolved. I have no other choice but to deal and by mid-November, things calm down just in time as the cold weather rolls in.

My parents take off for South Carolina and spend Thanksgiving and the entire month with my sister with no invitation for me. As usual, I try not to let it bother me.

Meg and I spent long afternoons at Hammonasset Beach State Park. It is the largest park in Madison, CT and has miles of pristine shoreline. Meg runs free on the beach because it's off season, and she has a ball.

There's other people around with their dogs, but they don't socialize much and nor do our dogs; I guess it's the Connecticut way.

Meg and I get used to not interacting with anyone and we keep to ourselves.

On our way home, we stop at Stop & Shop where I pre-order all of our groceries over an app and they place them into my car, and Meg doesn't have to sit alone and wait for me.

I get used to cooking for her and we both eat very healthy. She loves her spinach, broccoli and carrots which I serve her on a white Correll plate. She's treated like a queen.

We love walking in the neighborhood and the leaves are all but off the trees, and the ambiance is turning dismal and grey. The changing of the seasons is a glorious affair, and I have long forgotten about it but remember how beautiful it is now that I am living here again.

I continue to do loads of laundry in my new machines and keep everything clean. Soon, my place doesn't smell anymore and it's neat and orderly.

I upgrade all my cooking pans to steel and baking pans to glass to get rid of all things toxic.

I also buy the highest quality organic sheets for my bed and organic cotton and I sew my own pillows together, and I'm sleeping like royalty.

I upgrade all my towels and I go full monte and buy Matouk and I now have the fluffiest hand and face towels known to mankind. I even buy Italian, beautiful new rugs for my bedroom and living room that I can throw in my laundry machines. It is luxury supreme.

I purchase six different lilac trees from Home Depot and when they come, I plant them outside in the ground around my house before the snow falls, so they can sprout in the spring.

Meg is a big help by helping me dig the holes.

After Thanksgiving, Meg and I drive out to Clinton where we cut down our own Christmas tree!

We find the smallest one and a man who works there helps us chop it down with Meg staring over his shoulder.

It's in a field of thousand of trees, and people from all over the state come here to cut theirs down.

It's a festive affair and they have hot chocolate for the children and a gift shop. There's a lot of people, and it's a fun day.

We drive home with the Christmas tree jammed in the back seat of the car, and we're excited to set it up.

I had brought my aunt to the Dollar store last week when I was visiting her up at the convent, and she helped me pick out some of our Christmas tree ornaments.

I hang them up with Meg and then snap photos of her sitting underneath our Christmas tree. I even hang her own stocking!

It's the first time in my life I have ever had my own Christmas tree. *Never too late!*

And it's wonderful!

Chapter 42

Meg makes it all worthwhile! It is her first Christmas, after all.

She's so excited and with her big tail wagging, she knocks over the Christmas tree numerous times. I mop up the water that goes everywhere, but it does not dampen our spirits.

We are together, we are in love, and we have our own Christmas tree in our new New England home!

We snuggle up under the blankets and I light some candles giving the ambiance of a fireplace! I also bake banana bread in my new pans and we couldn't be happier!

Paradise and peace at last!!!!

Forty-Three

Chapter 43

❧⟨❀⟩❧

Christmas comes fast and my parents are back in town and nobody knows what the plans are until the last minute.

I like to know what we're doing and I don't want to have to go to the busy store at the last minute to get items they tell me to bring.

My cousin, Emma, decides or rather insists, to host the holiday at her house in Hartford.

I dread driving there in the snow, but my father is adamant that I come.

I have no heat in my car, and Meg and I freeze on our way up there.

The roads are slippery and filled with black ice and this is not fun for me.

My mother is already ranting about stuff like, "Don't bring the dog," and when that doesn't go well for her, she insists I bring the chain to, "Leave the dog outside."

Yes. In zero degree weather.

We drive up and I need to go to the bathroom BAD so on the way when we pass the Marriott Wallingford, I decide to go in and use it.

Meg waits in the car because she has since been ban from the hotel.

I know it was because the poor thing had her period and there was blood on the sheets that I couldn't get out.

I had decided, after thorough research, that I was not going to get her spayed.

I was not having her undergo major surgery to take her uterus out so she wouldn't get pregnant.

You avoid getting pregnant by not having sex, plain and simple. She was not allowed to sleep with other dogs unless she was married. LOL.

And after learning that in countries like Germany and Scandinavia, it's considered unethical and known as castration, I blew the whole thing off.

I'm sorry, I just wasn't putting her through that.

Her chance of getting cancer wasn't really that high and they don't tell you about the long-term risks where some studies show a potential increase for certain orthopedic conditions like hip dysplasia which is common in German Shepherds.

I'm glad I did my own research and made my own informed decisions because after Covid, I hardly trust the medical community anymore.

Meg waits in the car and I'm back in less than two minutes, and we are back on the road again to my cousin's.

When we arrive, it's impossible to get up the hill to her house without slipping, and it is FREEZING COLD OUTSIDE, and truly, I just long for my California Christmas' days spent alone on the beach in the beautiful weather watching the waves.

We get inside and thank God for Meg because she is the life of the party and my cousin allows her to stay inside the house which is really nice and her house smells like pretty pumpkin candles and it's warm and cozy.

Her boyfriend, Ray Ray, is cooking up all the food, but nothing is coming out of the kitchen fast enough, and everybody is starving.

My father looks like he could die of starvation at any minute because he's so skinny and so is my mother for that matter, and it's getting annoying.

My cousin, Louis, is here from Arizona, and as usual, he keeps asking where the wine is, and when the bottle appears on the table, he keeps asking for more.

No surprise there.

As he gets sloshed, I start to make jokes about where the f*ing food is, and I am told that "Ray Ray is handling everything."

So I say, "Wow, he is such a doll. Ray Ray, if you're ever single again, hit me up."

My cousin Louis, who is more sloshed now, busts out laughing, and my Aunt who's deaf keeps asking what's so funny.

Louis repeats it, and we all start laughing harder and I think this is why my cousin blows me off forever after this.

It was a *joke*.

Her boyfriend is *not* my type and when have I ever had a boyfriend anyway, so it's just a long day, and I can't wait until I'm home again with Meg back underneath the blankets.

The musty smell of my house still hits me in the face when

I get home, and I wonder if the mold is really, truly gone.

I start to sour on this whole idea of living here because my mother still can't stand me, my father is caught in the middle, I really don't have any relationship with anybody here in Connecticut, the cold weather KILLS MY ARTHRITIS, and I just feel like it's all for naught.

Meg and I ring the New Year in alone and I vow to get us out of this mess.

How, I do not know, but I have to figure something out.

Have to.

Forty-Four

Chapter 44

❧❦❧

The long winter weather wrecks havoc on my physical, mental and spiritual health.

There's days I love; like staying home in my house clothes, baking, and the first snow fall when everything turns white and the glistening snow muffles the world in silence and all comes to a standstill.

I snap photos of this winter wonderland and send them to my mother.

She responds with, "Wait until you can't walk on the black ice when the snow doesn't melt and it turns black from all the dirt and filth."

It's not the response I'm expecting, but I must hand it to her, she ends up being right.

The first few walks with the dog are a blast; throwing snowballs, kicking up the snow in the air with my boots, and watching Meg run around in it, but then it just becomes too much.

We slip, fall down, she's cold, and I'm irritable.

I buy her an adorable pink jacket and she looks beautiful in it, but I'm wearing so many clothes, I can hardly move.

I go outside buttoned-up to the gills, three scarves, two winter hats over a baseball cap, large sunglasses to shield my eyes, and a North Face coat. I got it years ago when I worked on Wall Street and paid a small fortune for it. I thought I'd be going skiing but I was never a skier, so I lugged it around with me all over California, and now, it has finally found its use.

My mother says she has a "whole bunch of my winter coats that she's going to give me," but this never happens.

The treacherous weather prevents me from going to the convent and seeing my aunt and from getting Angie's groceries at the food bank, which I've been doing bi-weekly.

It feels like winter is never going to end.

The heat doesn't work right and I'm always worried that this "gas," which I have never had to use before in my life is unhealthy and leaking and it's going to kill me, so I rarely use it. The cheap windows never keep the cold air out and there's ice on the windows, and in a word, it's awful.

I buy a "heat healer," on sale for my arthritis which costs $600, and it's like a giant sleeping bag sauna. You turn it on and then crawl into it for an hour and it gives off infrared light and heals your bones.

I close my eyes and pretend I'm on a hot beach in California, preferably Malibu, listening to the waves. It brings me insurmountable peace.

I also take up baking. I bake everything under the sun in my new pans – muffins, cinnamon buns, banana bread, apple crumb bread, even focaccia bread and it all comes out excellent.

I put most of it in the freezer to save for my parents, but it all goes bad because I never get to see them. When I tell them I'm taking a drive up, they always "have plans."

Meg loves my delicacies and I have non-toxic toaster ovens that I heat everything up in for her. We try to make the best of it, but by April it's still freezing and the same with May.

June arrives and there seems to be no spring at all – just heat and humidity that's unbearable.

Meg stops taking walks with me; she just can't hack it. I leash her up, take her out of the house, but she stands in the front yard and refuses to go further.

Plus, there's the bugs.

Oh, God, there's bugs everywhere, not to mention *the ticks*.

My allergies give me constant problems; I love to read, but the film over my eyes makes everything blurry and I'm getting weird headaches.

I thought I'd begin to see my parents more during the warmer months or I'd want to get out and about more, but it never happens.

My parents never want to see me; they make every excuse on the planet, and I begin to resent the whole thing.

I lost my California tan and California sparkle, and I just want it all back.

But how?

I wonder if I could ever go back to that apartment-style living. Now that I'm living in a house and have a dog, things are different.

To let Meg out to go to the bathroom by simply clicking her onto a chain in the front yard is bliss in comparison to having to leave an apartment and walk down three flights of stairs.

Plus, there's no noise, no interruptions. I have no shared walls; no one above me or below me, and to sleep solidly throughout the night is the greatest gift of all.

I feel so much better.

Also, to do laundry in my brand new washing machine and dryer is a blessing. Not to have to get into an elevator or lug dirty laundry down three flights of stairs to a basement and use public laundry machines, makes me NEVER want to go back to that life ever.

With a dog, everything gets dirty all the time, especially my rugs. To be able to throw them in the machine, and have my whole house smell like clean laundry detergent is something I love.

Yes, there's a lot to love.

But also, there's a lot to be weary of. It's affordable housing and the neighbors are weird. When Meg stops walking with me, there's a long stretch of road that's just forest, and anybody could be waiting for me and grab me and take me into the woods.

One time, when I saw a random car parked on the side of the road that I have never seen before, I went to a neighbor's house down on the main road and had them call the police. They came out immediately and took care of it.

I don't like taking chances like this.

But I'm still taking chances in the market and it's a worthless cause because the Fed has cranked up this market to all-time highs, and there's no volatility. It has become the scam of all scams and everybody knows we're in a huge bubble.

I start to wonder what my long term options are, especially in this financial predicament, and for once, I cannot foresee my future.

Everything seems muddy. Distorted. Like I have lost my way.

Lost my compass in life.

This is not a long term fit.

But what's next?

Can I really risk it and hit the road again?

With Meg?

Forty-Five

Chapter 45

My father pulls his Mercedes up in the driveway next to mine, and Meg starts barking.

I look up from my heat healer, and check the time – he's fifteen minutes early, as usual. He's over an hour away from me in Connecticut, and I guess he raced here. Anxious, discontent, wanting to flee my mother.

I crawl out of the heat healer, and I'm lightly covered in sweat. I'm wearing sweatpants that have holes in them and a warn out t-shirt.

I wanted to be clean and showered and presentable by the time he arrived, but no such luck.

I look as horrible and as warn out as I feel and I hardly care. That's when you know it's bad, when you stop caring.

"Daddy, daddy," I sing, wrapping him in a big hug. He enters the house and Meg is barking up a storm and she still doesn't know who he is.

He's wearing a baseball cap and a preppy Champion wind jacket and he pawns the dog off of him. "Don't have the dog jump on me, please Julie, please, come on."

Julie is what he calls me when he's mad. And he has plenty reasons for being mad, first and foremost the two hundred and fifty thousand dollars in debt he's paid since I arrived in Connecticut.

"Dad, how are youuuuuu?! I've missed you!!!!" I reach up to kiss him and Meg is jumping all around, excited and enamored.

But my father is holding a paper cup with coffee in it and I can't wrap my arms around him. Plus, Meg is coming between us, trying to tear us apart.

"Julie, the DOG!" my father says again. "Don't let him rip my jacket!"

It's a *her*, but she looks like a *him*, because she's such a big, fierce German Shepherd. I watch as she reaches her tan paws up on him.

I giggle, because she's getting so big and she's such a love bug. "Meg, get off Gramps! He's tired, he just had a long drive."

Meg starts panting and turning around in circles. She knows I'm happy, and I'm very happy now, I'm so glad my father came to visit me.

"Where's the coffee?" he asks.

"Dad, relax, I just got out of the heat healer, I need to take a shower and you got here early."

"Put the dog out!" he exclaims.

"Okay, Dad, I will. I'll put her out for a minute while you get settled."

I grab the cable that's stuck in the ground outside. Meg likes to roam the front yard, and I don't do this in the mornings, because you have trash men coming, and the mailman and the Amazon delivery guys. She hates the Amazon guys. Plus, she's like Houdini, she can wrestle out of her collar and run off, which she is known to do.

Luckily, because I live on a dead end street, and it's not that bad. *Yet.* Although we have had some incidents.

I get my father situated in the comfortable wicker chair whereby I hand made new cushions and threw out that toxic fake polyester crap that comes from overseas, and it's like sitting on a cloud.

Handing my father the remote control for my TV, I tune it into CNBC, and make my way into the shower.

"How was the drive, Dad?" I call. "I'll be right out, just need a quick shower. I love you!" I repeat. "I'm so glad you're here!"

I quickly clean myself and put on lipstick and a pair of yoga tights and a clean white T-shirt with an oversized flannel shirt over that.

It's June but still freezing in Connecticut and the weather here blows.

I attach hair extensions onto the massive pile of my blond hair and I put a big bow in my hair.

I look pretty. I will always be pretty, I think, as I stare at myself in the mirror looking at my big green eyes which don't even require makeup.

I make my way out to the living room, and my father seems more relaxed now than he was when he arrived.

I bring the dog in, but keep her attached to my desk so she can't pawn at my father, and I start making the coffee.

Meg is staring at my father, and then she looks back at me. It's like she's saying, "Are we good, Mom? Are you okay with him being here?"

I pat her head, assuring her everything is okay.

Still, she is on high watch.

I grind the coffee beans and as I do, he is rushing me. "I just want you to warm up my cup."

"Dad, I'm going to make fresh coffee, relax."

At eighty-four years old, he's still in a hurry. I don't know where he thinks he's going. Life, when not working, seems to come to a complete standstill.

Since I took disability, every day feels like ground hog day with watching the market, waiting for a crash so I can pay off my father, and trying to start a new life.

As the espresso comes pouring out of my new machine in the tiny little adorable espresso cups that I just purchased, I place them on a silver tray and carry them over to him.

"No! I don't want espresso, that's too strong. My stomach! Just hot coffee."

"Oh, okay, Dad, hang on."

I return to the coffee machine where I am brewing a fresh pot. It is not coming out fast enough, and I'm getting flustered.

The coffee beans and opened coffee bags are all over my kitchen counter and I like everything neat and clean, and everything is looking sloppy and unacceptable for my father.

Meanwhile, the dog is getting frantic, picking up on the bad vibes.

She starts jumping up and down on the leash which is attached to my desk chair, and she starts barking.

She rarely barks unless she sees somebody at the house which looks like a security threat, and she can't stand all my neighbors.

"My darling!" I coo. "That's Gramps! That's my father! You don't have to yell, my little love poo poo, ooooh, I love you

SO MUCH!"

I get on my knees and kiss her face as she keeps one eye on my father.

Watching.

"Come and sit with me," my father orders, as if he's always planning his escape out of here.

"Okay, dad, let me pour your coffee," I say. I bring his coffee cup to my machine and put milk in it.

When I bring it back over to him, he complains it's too much milk and now the coffee is cold.

I throw it out and start again, wasting a lot of coffee. Coffee is expensive, but once I make it just right and pour a cup for me, I sit down in the chair opposite him. "How's it going, Dad? I'm so glad you came."

"Yes," he replies. "It's so peaceful here."

"Yes," I agree. *Peaceful and boring.* I don't say that. He's well away how much I don't like Connecticut and how I want to return to LA, but he absolutely won't listen to any of that.

"How's Mom?" I ask, wishing I didn't the second the words fall from my lips.

He rolls his eyes. "Fine. She has so many health issues."

My mother is a real piece of work, and things just seem to be getting worse and worse by the minute. "I know, Dad, but why won't she let me help her? That's why I'm here. To be of service," I remind him.

"She doesn't need you now," he says, as he's done a million times before.

It's not that she doesn't need me, she *doesn't want me.*

I don't say this because I know it pains my father to see me in pain and my mother cause me nothing but that.

He thinks his money is the antidote to my pain, but it's not.

At this, our Mercedes outside glisten in the sun through the big window, and he asks, "How's the car?"

It's as if it's reminder that he just bought me that.

In outright cash. "It's great, thank you, Dad," I say.

Mercedes makes an incredible car. It's pure class and a grand improvement from the 1999 C class that I practically drove into the ground.

"Good," he says.

And as I look at him, he looks tired, distant. Defeated.

"Julie," he begins, "that dog, you know, she is tying you down. You can't go out, you can't do anything."

"Dad," I say in her defense, "she is my service dog, remember, I have arthritis."

"Julie, come on, she is like a ball and chain. You haven't met anybody, you don't have any friends. You don't go out. You just stay in with the dog all the time."

"Dad, we go out everywhere. We go to the beach, we go on walks, WE. ARE. FINE."

I look over at Meg who's just sitting there watching us. She starts trying to wrangle out of her leash. I get up to bring her some water hoping she's not thirsty.

She kisses me again as I bend down, and I pet her for relief. She knows I'm stressed now, and she's not happy.

She starts barking again.

"I don't know how you DO IT WITH THAT DOG!" my father yells.

"Dad, what are you talking about? Meg is no trouble! She's a dream boat."

"Put her in the cage!" he orders.

Suddenly, my childhood flashes before me. When I was distressed, it was "Go to your room!" When I got older it was,

"Put her in private school." When that didn't work out, it was, "Put her in therapy!" When that didn't work, it was, "Send her out of state to live with her grandparents!" When none of that worked, there was the *stick*. From the rocking chair.

Finally, I escaped at eighteen and never looked back.

Until now.

"Dad," I remind him, "Remember in the first few days when I got the dog, I thought of giving her back!? Do you remember?! And then I get a text out of no where from Mom. Do you remember what she said?"

He looks at me and shakes his head.

"She said," I say, raising my voice, "If you even THINK of giving that dog back, we will disown you."

"Oh, please," he says, "And when did you ever listen to her?!"

"What are you talking about, Dad? I always listen to her! I do nothing but TRY TO PLEASE HER!"

And there it is.

My words hang in the air.

Now Meg is really getting upset and I relent and put her back outside. "Just stay out here for a few minutes, darling," I say, "Okay? You can come back inside in a minute."

I leave the front door open so I can keep my eye on her and turn back to my father. He stares at CNBC not saying anything to me.

"Dad, I'm doing the best I can. We're happy, we're safe out here in Connecticut, and we're waiting for the market to crash so we can buy that second home in Florida. Right, Dad? Aren't we going to Florida this winter?"

My eyes plead with him.

Living on my $2670 monthly disability checks hardly accounts for a vacation home, let alone even basic living expenses for me and the dog.

"Yeah, yeah, sure, we'll go to Florida this winter..."

I can't tell if he's serious or trying to placate me.

The plan for me leaving LA and coming to the east coast was to become a homeowner. But housing has been sky high and we won't buy at these inflated prices.

Further, I should not be needing my father to acquire any housing for me, especially since he just paid all that debt. I'm starting to feel overwhelmed and like a loser and I'm getting a headache.

"If only my screenplay sold in LA, Dad, I wouldn't be in this predicament."

"Shoulda, woulda, coulda," he mumbles, and even I can hear the disappointment in his voice.

At this, the mailman arrives and Meg starts barking. She's never outside when he comes and she's going crazy.

She is going absolutely ballistic, jumping up and down on the cable and pulling it and she's pulling it so hard, I'm worrying it's going to come out of the ground, and she'll escape.

I wouldn't blame her for trying to escape this drama right now.

I get up and call out to her, "MEG, calm down."

She doesn't listen to me. In fact, she's getting more and more riled up, the closer the mailman comes. "MEGGGGGG!" I call again.

The mailman comes closer and when he arrives in front of our house, Meg twists her neck and wrangles out of her collar, ESCAPING!

She chases after the mailman, and goes right up to the mail truck and jumps on it.

Chapter 45

The mailman stays stops and I swing open the screen door, and run outside. "Meg, Meg!!!!"

She is not coming towards me and she's going berserk.

The mailman stays stopped until I can get a hold of the dog.

I run back inside and grab her lease and her ball. "Dad!" I cry, "Help!!!! The dog has escaped!"

But I think my father has gone into the bathroom, and I race back outside.

"Meg! Come back!!!" I throw her ball in the opposite direction of the mailman and she chases it.

"I'm sorry about that," I say to him and run off to get the dog.

She's running in circles around the dead end street and thinks this is fun and a big game. "Dad!" I plead, "Grab the treats on the counter!"

But he never comes out and as the mailman drives off, Meg chases him down the street.

She is so far out of sight and she can run so fast, my heart starts racing.

I pray to God that she does not get run over. Cars go so fast down our dead end street and that dog has no fear.

I don't see her and I don't hear her and now I'm running and panic sets in. I am scared to death that I'm going to turn the corner and see her dead body lying in the street. And in this moment, my life flashes before me.

If anything happens to this dog, I wouldn't survive it. She is my responsibility. If I have to witness her in any pain or suffering, it will cut me and break me into a thousand pieces and I don't think I'd bounce back from it. Ever.

I pray and I pray and run and I run. "MEGGGGGGGGGG G!!!!!!!!"

An SUV passes me, and a guy calls out the window, "Hey, I just saw your dog."

I'm gasping for air, and suddenly I realize, in this moment, how happy I have been with this dog.

How, for all her work and trouble, she's been my rock. She has given me a purpose and a love that I have never known. An unconditional, deep, soulful love.

Please, God, I beg. As I have done so many times over this dog. *Please, let her be okay.*

And as I come running around the corner, there she is, coming straight towards me.

Her big red tongue is swaying from side to side, and she's got that devil's look on her face that I love. I quickly glance at her legs to see if she is bleeding or limping or hurt in any way.

She looks fine.

She follows me back into the house, and she's panting and frazzled and crazed. "What happened out there?" I ask, out of breath. "What happened?!"

My father comes out of the bathroom and says, "Put her in the cage!"

I want to SCREAM.

"This is our house, Dad! This is Meg's home. She lives here! She comes first. I am not putting her in the cage!"

My father sits back down, and Meg walks slowly in her cage and plops down. I bend down again to see if she is okay.

She looks fine.

I shut the door, and go outside to face my father again. "From now on, we can only talk weekly, okay?" he says. "No more emails, no more texts. Forget your mother. She's not going to come around."

"Okay, dad."

222

"Hang in there for six more months. In December, we'll get a rental in Florida and go for the winter."

"Sounds good."

I let Meg out of the cage and she sits down in front of my desk. I sit down beside her. "Are you okay, darling?"

When we sit beside one another, we are the same height.

She looks at me and kisses my face, and I throw my arms around her giving her the biggest bear hug that I can. I squeeze her tight and don't let go.

I bury my face in her fur, "I love you, my darling. I love you."

Forty-Six

Chapter 46

The Fourth of July rolls around and I get an invitation from a childhood friend who I spent nearly every summer with at the beach, Amy.

She was the oldest of four children and she had the greatest mom growing up. They practically took me in as a fifth child, and those were my best memories; the tiny, small private beach we spent our summers on: boating, swimming, and eating Oreo cookies and Ring Dings with my grandmother and grandfather and all our other relatives.

I had gotten Amy's phone number from one of Angie's friends, and when I called her, her voice sounded the exact same, and we talked as if no time had passed at all.

She tells me she's heading down to the private beach in Branford for the Fourth, where we grew up, and the plan was we would meet at one o'clock.

She informs me "everyone will be there," and it will be

"packed," and "fun."

I wonder if my childhood crush, Chris, her cousin, will be there but when I ask her about him over the phone, she says, "He's married." I don't think she ever knew about the crush I had on him.

I call Angie, who always complains how she's "alone during the holidays," and tell her I'll pick her up and take her to the beach.

She's excited, and the next day, I put on my prettiest white eyelet sun dress and make my way over to her place at 1:15.

I arrive on time and help Angie into the car with her beach chair, her walker, and the cooler she's bringing along.

When we get the beach, it's packed. I pull my car over to the side of the road to help Angie with all of her things, and when I look around our old beach in the old neighborhood, I don't recognize anyone.

I try, naturally, to find all my old relatives, but I realize most of them have passed away. *Years ago.*

It's a very strange feeling. I immediately miss my grandmother. And my grandfather. And the way it was. And the life I once had here.

I'm standing there with Meg, who's ready to charge for the water, and Angie, who's weak and frail and needs to sit down.

Everyone sits in cliques.

They turn, one by one, to look at us.

It is obvious I don't live here or belong here anymore. A void envelops me. I feel uncomfortable. I stand there looking stupid and I don't know what to do.

But I remember I have my dog and Angie to tend to, and this is not about me anymore. "Is Amy here?" I ask, to anyone who will listen.

No one answers.

Louder I ask, "Hiii everyone, do you where Amy is?"

"Amy who?"

Amy who? Wow.

I guess it's only been, what, forty years, since we ruled this place? It was our beach. With our boats. And our relatives and friends.

And now I know no one.

I say her full name and somebody points.

I have no idea who she's pointing to.

The dog is getting restless and the ninety-five year old looks like she's going to keel over.

Suddenly, there's my friend, Amy.... walking towards me. I see her and I get teary. Her face looks exactly the same, and she's smiling. She used to be a little chubster growing up, but her body is lean and she's beautiful. She always was beautiful, on the inside and out.

She wraps me in a huge hug and I'm still holding the dog and Angie's stuff, and I get emotional.

I feel lightheaded like I'm going to faint. I start crying and I'm so grateful I'm wearing sunglasses so nobody notices.

Amy senses this, and like a good friend, she helps me with the dog and gets Angie settled.

I leave with Meg to go park my car in front of my uncle's house up the street, which is right next door to my grand-mother's old house, and I make my way back down to the beach with the dog.

When Amy sees me, she suggests we go for a walk, and together, to get away from that packed beach, we walk along the shore.

We can't catch up fast enough and it feels so good to see her again. "So you got married, twice?!" I ask her.

"Yeah, yeah," she says, but she's more interested in my life.

"Amy, wait a minute! And you have four kids?!"

"Yep."

"Four boys, but one is transitioning."

"Transitioning?" I ask.

"Yes, he's going to be a girl."

I turn to look at her, and it seems that she doesn't want to discuss it. We both come from conservative families and I'm surprised. "Well, at least now you'll have a daughter! That's great!!"

She laughs a little. "Yeah. So tell me about you, come on!"

"Amy, I don't know, after eighteen years in LA, the adjustment to Connecticut hasn't been easy. The changing of the seasons and adapting to this weather is hard. And the cold winters... the tics in the summer..."

Was it this bad when we were they're growing up? Did things change? *Or were we just too young and naïve to notice?*

As we both ramble on, we agree on how much the neighborhood has changed. Houses are uber expensive and they're growing so big that they're on top of each other. Taxes are sky high, not to mention, the "hurricane insurance."

Amy is lucky that her family kept all their houses here, and they even bought more when people died. They're now worth a pretty fortune.

It seems to be the spot to be now, but when we were growing up, it was just our little secret place that nobody knew about... where we'd ride our bikes, rollerskate, and go out in the row boats to the Thimble islands, and jump off divers rock.

We'd sit in the sun all day, make sandcastles, and wait for the ice cream man to come. Then, we'd go back up to the house, use the outdoor shower to wash off, and my grandmother would have a massive Italian meal ready.

Good times. Life will probably never be that good again.

Meg hurries along the street, sniffing everything, and she yanks me on the leash, yanking me back into the here and now.

She grounds me, because right now, the world and all the people in it, seem to be up in the air, and I am looking up at the sky with a million questions that may or may not ever get answered.

When we get back to the beach, Meg wants to go running in the water but the beach is packed, and Amy is adamant that it's not allowed.

Angie is hot and wants to go, and I don't get to see any of Amy's kids, or her sister's kids, or her cute cousin Christopher, and the next thing I know, we're back in the car, going home.

Angie tells me what a great time she had and thanks me for taking her. She knew a lot of people, and this really is a small town where everybody seems to live here their whole lives.

I get home, my head is spinning, and I need to eat and use the bathroom, and when I finally sit down, I'm alone again and it's quiet.

I listen to the people outside in my neighborhood carry on with their Fourth of July festivities with their big families, I realize I once had that life here, and it was a great life, but those old days are no more.

I feel homesick for the old version of my life which doesn't exist anymore.

It is very humbling to see the way life just goes on. People die, people move, new people come and are born, and the world changes.

Whether I like it or not.

Forty-Seven

Chapter 47

Three days after the Fourth of July is my birthday. I decide that it's Meg's birthday too, since the rescue agency didn't know when her real birthday was, and I'm excited to celebrate.

I was never one to make a big fuss on my birthday; I'd always just spend it alone quietly, doing something I loved. But today, that's not our fate because my parents are blowing into town to take us to lunch.

At 10:30 a.m.

STAT.

"Why can't we meet in Westport?" I asked when receiving my mother's text of, "We're going to Bill's in Westbook for lunch on your birthday. Look it up."

When I looked it up on the map, I realized it was thirty minutes away from me in the OPPOSITE DIRECTION of my parents, which meant it was two hours away from them.

My eight-five year old parents!

"Are you getting a hotel?" I ask.

I didn't want to be difficult, I'm grateful to spend the day with them, but now I'm starting to think my mother is losing her mind.

On the text chain with my parents, out comes a quick response from my father, "No."

"Why are we going so far?" I ask again.

It makes no sense. I get no response and accept this is my fate.

I have no say, nor will I ever have any say, when it comes to making plans with my mother, and she one hundred percent, controls my father.

The morning of my birthday, I wake up later than usual at 8:00 a.m., and I have things to do before they arrive.

I want to go running, walk the dog, clean the yard and bathroom, and have coffee ready for my father on time.

I hurry out of bed and I only get a few minutes of meditation in, before I need to get going. As I push myself to run, not only do I feel the pain from my arthritis, but I feel more mental pain at the idea of seeing my mother.

Maybe when I get home, I will get a text saying they can't come.

But maybe today, won't be so bad, my other side argues.

Maybe it'll be wonderful. Where we are all in love, having great conversation, and acting like normal people.

When I get home, I quickly strap the leash on Meg and say, "Let's go sweetheart." We embark on a quick "gang walk," and this is by far, the best part of my day.

Although I'm inpatient when she stops to sniff something because we don't have time. We get home, I clean the kitchen, the bathroom, prepare the coffee, wash fresh blueberries, and put two of my homemade muffins in the toaster oven.

From there, I shower and put on a pretty dress and makeup.

I am exhausted before they even arrive.

My sister sends me a happy birthday text and says, "I'm around to talk in the morning if you have time."

I have no desire to speak to her.

Whoever abandoned you in the middle of the ocean has no right to know what the sharks did to you or how you managed to the shore.

But when my mother texts me that they're running late, I go ahead and take the bait.

"How's it going, Julie?" I hear her ask into the phone, in that same childlike voice that irks me.

"Great," I utter, "Just great! Mom and Dad are on their way over for my birthday."

I look out the window and check the balcony to see if I remembered to put up the iron gate so Meg can stay out there when they arrive. I did.

"Are they?" she quips.

"Yep, can't wait," I respond with a hint of sarcasm.

It bothers me to have to speak to my sister so nonchalantly after she ignored me the entire year and a half that I lived in Mt. Pleasant. I am not one to sweep "issues under the carpet," yet this family is famous for it.

We start talking about writing which we are both passionate about, and my sister tells me she is still, "Waiting for the agents to respond to her query letters."

"The publishing industry is more manipulated than the medical industry or even Wall Street," I tell her. "Why are you depending on them? Just write the story you want to tell and self-publish."

"No, no," she replies, as if I am doing it all wrong.

We have nothing in common anymore, the dog starts barking, and my parents have arrived.

"I have to go," I conclude, "they're here."

"Have fun!" she chirps.

"Oh, I will!" I snap back, "Bye!"

My mother barrels through the front door, and she's carrying bags with junk falling out of them, and I try to help her, but Meg gets in the way jumping and barking.

"Mom, hiiii!! Can you hang on a second so I can put the dog out? You look great!" I say.

My mother ignores me.

Meg is barking and jumping and I try to control the dog, but my mother has no patience, and louder, I ask, "Mom, can you hang on?! I need to put Meg outside on the balcony."

Instead my mother walks right into Meg, who jumps right onto her tiny body and I get to hear her scream, "Oh, no! Julie! The dog! She just ruined my white pants!"

The day unravels from here.

Forty-Eight

Chapter 48

M y mother, bringing all this junk into my home, is acting like she's doing me a big favor, and my father plops down in the chair, exhausted and drained.

"Dad, are you okay?" I ask, "I could have come to Westport! I didn't want you to drive all the way here."

"That's okay, I didn't want you to drive," he musters.

"Dad, I made fresh coffee. It's all ready, let me get you a cup!"

"No coffee!" my mom orders. "It's bad for his stomach."

"Yeah, I'll take half a cup," my Dad says.

"Great, Dad, okay, should I heat up the milk?"

"Jerry, you're going to have to go to the bathroom! Do you REALLY NEED TO HAVE THAT COFFEE?"

I'm holding the pot, staring at both of them, not sure what to do or which will promote less of a rage out of my mother.

"I'm hungry," my mother says, "We need to EAT, JULIE!"

"Mom," I say, proudly pointing to my beautiful silver tray. "Here are heated homemade muffins and fresh blueberries from the farm..."

"We don't SNACK BEFORE lunch!" she snaps. "We're hungry!

"Can't we just relax a little? You just got here."

"No, we cannot! We have been sitting in that car and we need to move AROUND!"

I wish I never came back east. *When can I get back to California???? When???*

"Mom, are you sure you want to drive all the way out to Westbrook? It's far. It's going to take us at least thirty minutes to get there. Why can't we just go to the lobster place down the road?"

"I don't want a lobster roll!" she sneers, stomping her feet like a child.

She turns to my father, "Jerry! You said we could go to Bill's! We like that menu there and I want my fried clam strips!"

"Okay, okay," my Dad says.

He looks depleted. It's like there's not even a person there inside of him anymore; my mother sucks the life out of him.

I pour the coffee for my father, and he takes the cup from my hand eagerly. I also pour the milk in as I stand over him, careful not too pour too much.

"That's perfect," he says.

I carry over my silver tray to my mother, which also holds two small glasses of ice water. "Here, please help yourself. Have some water and a snack," I offer my mother again.

My mother pushes it away with a swipe of her hand. I bring it to my father, and he reaches for half of a blueberry muffin.

"I don't want A SNACK!" my mother keeps saying. "We don't EAT IN BETWEEN MEALS! We aren't like you, Julie, WE EAT LUNCH!"

"Okay, Mom," I relent, "Who's car are we taking and where are we going?"

"I want to go to Bill's! That was our plan!"

"Mom, it's very far."

"Jerry," she says, turning to him red faced. "You see?! I knew this was going to happen! This is EXACTLY WHY I DIDN'T WANT TO COME!"

"Mom, if you don't mind sitting in the car for another forty minutes, I'll drive. But there's a restaurant that's closer in Madison that has clam strips, so maybe we can go there."

"Okay, let's go," she spews.

All the hot coffee I prepared and the muffins are all going to go to waste now, and I have to pack up the dog, get her water, her leash, and all the stuff out of the back seat of my car so my parents can squeeze in.

This all takes about fifteen minutes with my mother standing out in the heat, huffing and puffing.

I'm already disappointed, and can't even believe this is my "wonderful birthday."

We take off, the dog is in the front seat with me, my parents are in the back, and no sooner than twenty minutes into the drive, there's construction on the Post Road and we're re-routed.

My mother thinks I'm taking "the scenic route," and starts yelling. "Why is this taking so long?! Why, Julie!? Where are you TAKING US?!"

"Mom, we just got re-routed from the road construction. Didn't you see all the men in the road?"

My Dad is in the backseat, silent, knowing not to get involved The less he says, the better.

"I'm getting hungry, this is taking forever," my mother keeps saying over and over again like a problem child.

"We're almost there, Mom, hang on," I croon in my sweetest voice, trying to console her.

She rolls her eyes, and we make it back onto the Post Road from the re-route.

Now nobody can find the restaurant.

I guess it's been closed down and renamed since they grew up in this area in what, *over SIXTY YEARS ago?!*

"There it is!" my Dad says, but I don't think he has any idea what he's talking about.

The restaurant has a sign that says, "Fish," and I think he will just do anything to get out of the car.

I egg him on. "That looks great, Dad!" I say, "Wow, that didn't take long at all," I add, lying.

We all make our way out of the car.

"Go get us a table, Julie, someplace far away so the dog doesn't bother anybody and we'll come out and find you."

The place is completely empty, but I say, "Okay, Mom."

I find a table way in the back, sit down with Meg, tie her to a picnic table, and say, "This is almost over, honey, just hang in there."

My parents come back out with the food. There's two humongous lobster rolls sitting on the tray for me and my father, and my mother has her fried clam strips.

"Wow! Thanks, Dad! That looks delicious!"

He nods, and I'm sure can't wait until this is over.

When my mother goes to sit down at the picnic table, she yells, "This seat is filthy! I can't sit on that!"

I had brought a small dish towel that I had in the car for the dog, so I offer it to her. "Here Mom, you can sit down on this. You'll be fine."

She nixes under her breath and sits, but not before adding, "Make sure that dog doesn't come anywhere NEAR ME!"

The picnic table is huge and we don't have any problems.

I dig into the lobster roll and it's outstanding; succulent lobster meat served on a split-top hot dog bun that is buttered and toasted and golden brown. "Wow, Dad, it's incredible!"

Is it worth the aggravation of sitting with my mother and driving all the way down here?

Absolutely not.

My mother starts complaining about the sun in her face and says she needs to move picnic tables.

We all get up and move, and I have to untie and retie the dog again to another table. Then my mother says, "I don't like the clam strips."

I look up, hoping I'm imagining it. "What?"

"I don't like the clam strips!"

My dad doesn't say anything. I look at him in astonishment. "Let me try them," I reply.

My mother pushes the full plate of clam strips in front of me, and I dig in. Everything is as succulent as the roll and she also has fried onion rings, and I try those, and it's all delicious. "Mom, they're great. Why don't you like them?"

She doesn't answer.

She turns to my father while eyeing the ice cream stand. "Can we get ice cream?"

We haven't even finished our lunch and now she wants ice cream.

"Sure," he says, and I wonder how many ice creams the

poor man had to buy this monster in his lifetime. Probably thousands.

"I'm lactose intolerant!" my mother spews, "I'm just thinking of the two of you!"

"I'm good," I say. "I don't want any."

"Neither do I," my father says.

"Oh, boy, you two really are something," my mother splutters with pure vile and hatred in her voice. "This is why I didn't want to come! This is WHY!"

I look at her amazed as she punches the table with her fist. "You NEED HELP, JULIE!"

I am grateful no one is around us.

"You NEED IT BAD!" she adds.

My father seems unfazed by all of this, as if this is just "another day in his life," and I can't wait to leave.

The day drags on and on, my mother never gets her ice cream, and when they're finally leaving my house on a day that feels like it's never going to end, my mother turns to my father and says, "I sucked it up for her birthday, and THIS IS WHAT I GET, DISRESPECT!"

Adios.

Don't come back.

I shut the door.

And try to quiet my brain from wanting to off myself.

Forty-Nine

Chapter 49

I wake up to a spotless home the next morning because I spent the last four hours yesterday fumigating the place, and cleaning out the toxicity from of parents being there. I also ran a Tarot because this is the end of the road.

I've been on the East coast for three years and three months now, and things haven't gotten better, only worse.

My health is deteriorating, I'm going to implode from Lyme disease if I don't have it already, and I need to get out of Dodge.

I ask the Tarot what the future holds, and for the first time in a long time, I feel hopeful.

I feel like this is a bottom, and things can only go up from here.

The Tarot card I pull is the seven of disks. *The failure card.* I lie in bed confused and baffled.

The failure card is significant. But sometimes, failures are good. Failures take you in a different direction. But since I

239

have Meg, I can't just jump on a plane and escape. I can't fly back to LA, and I don't have enough money to move.

Plus, I don't think I could abandon my father.

I want to be boots on the ground for him, because no matter how much I hate Connecticut, I love my father more.

So I decide that I need to create some boundaries to protect myself from the insanity, because if I am disgruntled, the only person I have to blame for that, is myself.

I create a beautiful sanctuary for Meg and I. First I make a herb concoction and I smother the herbs together in my clay crusher, make an intention, and then douse the herbs around my home by the windows, and I even sprinkle some outside the front door.

Protection.

Make no mistake about, this works.

And for the rest of the summer, Meg and I engage in a nice routine. I am working in the mornings, writing again, and this helps me. It's cathartic. Although I cannot do much with my arthritic fingers, I do what I can, and the release in the escape of it all, is life saving. I love the art of story, and I have so much content from all the stories of my past, I can spend the rest of my days holed up inside, working on books. It's love, it's bliss, it's my passion.

On the weekends, Meg and I go on adventures by visiting new places along the Connecticut shoreline; beaches we haven't been to, new parks, and the beautiful Mercy by the Sea in Madison, Ct. which is a retreat center.

One weekend we took a ride to Chester for a dog festival. We saw an old run down train pass by us, and we went to the oldest operational ferry in the United States. Also, we visit my aunt in the convent regularly, and I take her out to different farms where we sit outside on a blanket and drink "fake wine," which she loves, but cannot have, so I substitute cranberry juice, and we go into New Haven for the best pizza in the country and I even take her out to the shoreline for lobster rolls.

My aunt's health is deteriorating and it's sad to watch, but Meg keeps us happy and our spirits up. She is always such a happy, energetic dog. I love to watch Meg as she runs in the waves and does the doggie paddle at the beach, and she's always in her glory. She has a good life.

Correction, we have a good life.

Nothing gives me more happiness than to watch her, this beautiful German Shepherd, enjoy her good life. I finally understand what my father means when he says to me, "I just want you to be happy."

One Sunday, we take a beautiful, quiet walk in the neighborhood, and when we get home, I make us spinach and rice for dinner. Meg loves the cheese that I put on top of it, and she gobbles it right up.

I wait to sprinkle cayenne pepper all over it, which I believe has extraordinary health benefits, until the rice is cooked and I serve Meg hers first on her plate, because dogs can't handle the spices. Now, I am always cooking with her in mind.

We say Grace, and eat.

While I'm doing the dishes later, I let her out on the chain so she can go to the bathroom and I'm able to watch her from the kitchen window.

When I call her to come back inside, she's not coming, so I head to the front door to see what is going on.

Her face is buried underneath one of the lilac trees that we planted, and I see that she's chewing on something.

I get nervous, worrying that one of my neighbors left something poisonous on the ground for her to eat. They haven't taken a liking to the dog, and they resent her barking when strangers come to the dead end street.

I race outside, and she has gotten herself into an animal hole and I hear some kind of small animal whimpering.

I forgot to put on my glasses, and I cannot see what it is.

When I look closer at Meg, there's some sort of animal inside her mouth and I shout. "STOP!!! MEG STOP!!! PUT THAT DOWN!!"

But she only chews harder and she has this wicked look on her face.

One I have not witnessed before. She looks possessed.

I try to claw her mouth open, but she won't have it.

She chomps down harder and escapes me even though she is on the chain.

She knows one ninety degree turn of her neck and she can wrestle out of her collar and escape, and she gives me those eyes, *like Mom, stay back or this will get much, much worse.*

I run back inside and get her harness and her leash and I snap it on, and start to pull her, "GET IN THE HOUSE NOW, MEG!!! NOW!!!"

Whatever animal carcass that's in her mouth drops, and after a long struggle, I wrestle her back into the house and I am livid.

And in one solid second, I have turned into my mother.

"God damn you, Meg, GOD DAMN IT!!!!!" I have no idea what she ate, our grass is covered in pesticide from the exterminator who handles our massive Connecticut tick problem, and I am about to lose it.

Meg runs into her cage, knowing she did something bad

and that I am mad. I close her in there and take a shower to wash all the dirt that is now all over me from wrestling her outside.

I am sick to my stomach, and I call the police to see if animal control can come out.

I feel sorry for any animal who is out on my lawn suffering, half dead because of Meg, my wild beast of a dog decided it would be fun to destroy it.

They tell me animal control doesn't work on Sundays and won't be in until tomorrow at 7 a.m., and they say I can call back.

I let Meg out of the cage and call Lorna. She says, "They're dogs. They are predators. They chase and eat things. That's how they're wired."

"Do I need to call the vet?"

"Nah," she tells me, "she has her shots, just keep your eye on her."

"Okay, thanks, Lorna. Love ya," I hang up and am still worried.

I let Meg out of the cage. She looks at me with eyes that say, "I can kill things with my teeth. I can eat them alive. So watch it, Mom. You don't know my strength."

She looks tough as she continues to stare at me.

Her deep brown eyes peel into mine, "So watch it, Mom. I am a German Shepherd. And don't you forget it. And all those little fucks around here better not forget it either."

For a second, I am scared of her.

I'm scared of my own dog.

And in a strange way, I have a newfound respect for her.

During the night before when it was thundering, I had to get on my hands and knees and hold her again when she was hiding in her cage from the storm. I had to say over and over again, "Honey, don't be afraid, it's just thunder. It's okay, my love."

And now I am afraid.

Of *her*.

I ignore Meg for the rest of the night.

I just go through the motions of letting her out, pulling her away from the scene of the crime when she tries to go back over there, and then we go to bed in our separate areas.

The next morning, I can't call animal control fast enough.

I explain what happened to our Animal Control lady, Kelly, who has been out here before for the woodchuck issue, and she's over in a jiffy.

I'm standing outside with a shovel and gloves on, trying to look like I know exactly what I'm doing.

When she arrives, I leave Meg is inside the house, and Kelly inspects the area, and I just can't look.

I stand about twenty feet away from her with my back towards her. "Is there anything there?!" I blast. "Do you see any dead animals?!"

"I don't really see anything," she replies, as she circles the area.

"How about any dead animal carcasses?"

"Nope, I don't see a thing..."

"Really?" I ask in a surprised tone. "Are you sure? Can I come over?"

"Yep. There's nothing here."

"But that hole," I point as I come closer, "You see that animal hole, her face was down in that. What is it?"

Kelly looks closer and takes my big shovel and begins breaking apart the hay and soiled long grass, "Ohhhh, I see."

She keeps breaking it apart with my shovel. "It's a bunnies nest."

"A bunny's nest?"

"Yep."

"The bunnies live over there," I tell her, pointing to the tree in the middle of the roundabout in our road.

"Well, they built a nest right here," she says, and as she takes it apart, I hold open the cover of the trash for her while she throws it inside.

"Thank you," I tell her. "I really appreciate this, really, great work, thank you so much for coming out."

My heart is racing, and can't help but wonder if Meg slaughtered a baby bunny with her teeth.

"Can I get you something, Kell? A bottle of water or a lemonade?"

"No, no, I'm fine," she says. "Just put some dirt over there to cover that hole, and you should be fine."

"Okay, will do, thanks."

Kelly leaves, and when I go back inside, I take a look at the dog.

She is just staring at me like, "What? Do you have a problem?"

Yes, I have a problem. You do not kill wild things with your teeth.

She needs to be cleansed.

I need to set an intention with this dog, because resentments are like weeds; if you don't clip them at their root, they just continue to grow and fester.

I know if I didn't forgive this dog, right here and right now, every bad little thing that she does going forward will just turn into a hysterical reaction from me.

As they say, if its hysterical, it's historical.

245

I gather together my spice crusher, a white candle, a photo of Meg that's on a mug my cousin got me for Christmas, and I mix together thyme and crystallized salt.

I close my eyes and then I sit on the floor with the dog, and, as I crush the herbs and light the candle, I say a prayer, "By my word, I heal all that ails. No sickness may live, In this that I love."

I place the salt and Thyme mixture on Meg's forehead and her paws.

She sits still looking at me.

"From now on Meg you are not to interfere with nature. You are to mix with our surroundings and never interfere with the wildlife outdoors again. Do you understand? You are never, ever to harm another animal again. You are to live among nature and respect it ALWAYS."

I douse her with the herbs and wave my hands over her body.

She waits patiently until I am finished.

I close my eyes and repeat the words, "You are now cleansed. I forgive you, my love. So mote it be."

I blow out the candle and it's done. I will never bring up this incident again.

But I will always remember what happened.

And I will never forget that I am living with an animal who can cause death with her teeth.

And it can happen at *any time.*

Fifty

Chapter 50

During everything that happened yesterday with animal control and Meg, I reached out to my father. I haven't heard a response from him or my mother to any of my emails, and I have been keeping my distance since my whole birthday escapade, but now I was wondering if something was wrong.

I send out a blast email subtly explaining what happened to Meg the night before, and I get a reply first thing in the morning from my father, ignoring the incident with Meg, but explaining how my sister just blew into town with her family.

He informs me that she wants to see my aunt at the convent and for me to, "Make arrangements for this to happen," and he ends his email with, "CT is not the problem. The dog is not trained!!!" With explanation points, which my father never uses!!

I am irked to no end.

By A. his comment about the dog training And B. My sister is here and I better JUMP AT HER EVERY COMMAND.

When my dad calls me later on, he sounds frazzled. I can hear a lot of noise in the background and he sounds jumpy, "How's it going?" he asks.

"Going great, Dad," I reply, as if he has time for any of my problems.

"Did you hear back from Sister Victoria?"

"No, Dad, like I mentioned, I texted her yesterday reminding her of our family lunch next week and I wanted to see if the dates still worked, and I haven't heard anything."

"Well, can you try her again?"

"Dad, they're busy up up there at the convent," I stammer. "Sister Victoria has already done so much for me. If Sarah really want to see Auntie Jo at the convent and it was such a *priority,* she should have made her plans well in advance."

"Julie, there was a funeral for her friend's father, she came at the last minute, this was not planned! I told you that in the email!"

Oh, in the same way her last visit was a surprise visit?

She has these surprise visits as her passive aggressive way to have everyone jump at her every command. And I'm not falling for it.

At this point, I'm over this entire family.

"I don't know what to tell you, Dad," I say vaguely.

"Now Julie," he stammers, "your sister really wants to see Auntie Jo today. She's leaving tomorrow and Craig and Tommy are going into the city today and I'm taking them to the train station now."

WOW — MY POS brother in law would rather enjoy Manhattan then go with his wife to visit her ailing aunt in the convent who none of them have seen in what — ten years?!

I am beyond disgruntled by now.

"Dad, this is a lot of driving for you! Why do YOU have to drive them to the train station?! You're driving down here next week! That will be two trips for you in a matter of days!"

"Don't worry, I can handle it," he assures.

Why can't HER HUSBAND, (*HER LAZY ASS MOOCH OF A FUCKING HUSBAND, I WANT TO SAY, BUT HOLD BACK*) RENT A CAR AND THEY GO AS A FAMILY? Why do you have to take her?"

My father stutters back, "Oh, come on, Julie, just contact Sister Victoria, or I'll call her myself. We'll be there at 10:30 this morning, Sarah wants to see you, so meet us there."

I look at the clock.

It's already 8:30 a.m.

There's no way for me to clean up, get dressed, get the dog in the car and make it there by that time.

I am disabled and it takes a long time for me to get dressed. It's impossible for me to rush. Plus the dog still needs to run, and that can't happen with all the driving and packing up and I already had my coffee, so I can't stop at Dunkin' which makes the trip fun, and plus, my aunt looks forward to all the munchkins that I bring her, and it will look bad if I show up empty handed.

"Okay, Dad, I'll text Sister Victoria again now," I relent.

He doesn't even hear me. "Oh, I see them now at the edge of the parking lot! I have to go!" and my father clicks off.

"Hi Sister Veronica," I begrudgingly text, "My sister has come into town at the last minute for a funeral and would like to see my aunt this morning. Is this possible? I am sorry for the last minute notice."

She responds immediately. "That should be fine, Juliana."

I text back my father and let him know.

Then I put down my phone, and I stare out the window. I am suddenly filled with anxiety.

It'll be good to see my sister again, I think. *That's why I moved to the east coast.*

My other side argues. *The relationship with your sister is dead. She will only use and torment you.*

I start to get dressed anyhow. I hope for the best.

We are in a massive heat wave and it's already over 90*.

I let Meg outside and I decide to wash my car. She's sitting in the sun watching me and it looks like she doesn't want to go anywhere.

And truthfully, neither do I.

I re-evaluate the situation and decide that I'm going to hit traffic and the AC is barely working in the new car.

I go inside and text my father. "It's just too hot for Meg and we can't go. Sorry, Dad. Enjoy your stay with Auntie Jo and I will see her next week."

I add a little heart emoji and then I put on my running clothes and head out to walk Meg before the heat gets any worse and we run together to get out all the frustration.

When I get back home, I feel like I dodged a bullet.

If my sister really wanted to see me, why not contact me the SECOND SHE MADE HER PLANE RESERVATION? Give me more than a twelve hour notice! *Fuck all of them*, I think. With this, I call my mother.

Surprisingly, she answers. "Hi Mom!" I say, "How are you feeling?"

"I'm fine," she says curtly, "What's up?"

"Umm, I was just thinking, did Dad remember that there's

a train station in Ridgefield that he could drop off Craig and Tommy instead of taking them all the way to Westport?"

The Westport ride completely takes my father out of his way, but leave it up to all of them to put my father, my ELDERLY FATHER, last.

This sparks utter rage in my mother.

"Do not GET INVOLVED, JULIANA! YOU HAVE A VENDETTA AGAINST YOUR SISTER AND HER HUSBAND AND IT NEEDS TO STOP! WE DROVE DOWN FOR YOUR BIRTHDAY LAST MONTH BECAUSE YOU ASKED FOR IT AND NOW DAD IS DOING THE SAME FOR DEANA! MY HEART IS RACING! MY HEART! MY HEART!!!"

Unreal.

I cannot believe her words. "Mom, can you just calm down? I do not have a vendetta…"

"OH YESSS YOU DOOOOOOOO JULIE!!!!!! YOU MOST DEFINITELY DO! GET HELP! MY HUSBAND WILL DO WHAT HE WANTS! HE IS NOT YOUR HUSBAND! GET HELP!!!"

I wish I didn't call.

I cannot believe her rage.

My father was so wrong that this situation would get any better. It just gets worse and worse by the second.

I realize I'm not going to win or find any common ground with my mother EVER, and I just want to hang up without her dropping dead from a heart attack.

"Okay, mom, okay," I keep saying over and over again. "I love you, yep, yep, okay, talk to you soon. Bub – bye."

The temperature reads 85* in my house and it's not even 9:30 a.m. There is no central air here. There is no breeze, I can hardly breathe, and the humidity is off the charts. My allergies are acting up and I am putting up with disastrous living conditions to be close to my elderly parents and for what?

But then I remember....

That every problem in my life ...

Is from either a bad decision I have made, a decision I am avoiding, or a boundary, *I will not set.*

Fifty-One

Chapter 51

By August 1st, the heat wave breaks and Meg and I go to the park since it's cooler now, and then I need to head over to the jewelry store to pick up my diamond necklace that broke, after going to the food bank for Angie.

My necklace broke two weeks ago and it has been weird not seeing it hanging around my neck.

It was a gift from my ex-fiance when I was engaged in my thirties to the head trader at my work when I was living in Manhattan.

I called off the wedding two months before we were set to get married, and I returned the ring, but got to keep the necklace. It's a big diamond and I love it. It sparkles always.

I never take it off, and every time I look at myself in the mirror, though I'm seeing lines and wrinkles that have appeared on my face recently, the one thing that never fades is my sparkling jewelry.

My diamond studs earrings and necklace sparkle gloriously, and at this point, I too, am determined to get my sparkle back.

Meg and I arrive to the food bank early. I get Meg out of the car, and we head across the street to the huge fairgrounds. There's plenty of room for us to run there and play with her balls.

"Run freeeeeeee Meg!" I say when we arrive and unclip her leash. I throw the ball as far as I can, and we run like mad.

These are my happiest times.

Running with Meg in these huge fields that we find, far away from all humanity in nature.

I take her three balls out of my pockets, and keep throwing them. One ball is not enough for her, and she's so fast, she needs three to keep her going and run her ragged.

As I'm throwing, she is chasing and catching all the balls, while jumping in the air. I am so proud of her. Her agility and balance just astounds me.

Out of breath, we turn around and head back to the car where I have her gallon of cold water waiting.

As we meander down the street together, out of breath and spent, Meg hears gunshots go off, and so do I.

She looks back at me, like "Mom, what is that??!!!" She has that same look on her face when she runs for cover when she hears thunder.

"It's nothing, my love, don't worry."

But she won't have it.

As we pass a barn, she takes cover underneath it, crawling underneath the wood, and shields herself, refusing to come out.

I can't pull her, she is wrestling again, and she is about to come out of her harness which she knows how to do.

I get on my hands and knees, Meg is lying in dirt and filth, and I'm trying to yank her out to no avail. I get back up and look around, not knowing what to do. I throw her ball down the street and start chasing it on my own but she doesn't buy it and she won't come out.

We can't be late for the food bank or I'll miss the slot to get Angie's groceries.

Lost as to what to do, when I look around again, coming down the desolate street, is a young boy. He's carrying a phone and listening to ear buds.

I watch as he comes closer.

He's about ten years old and adorable. "Hiiii," I say in somewhat of a panic, "I need help!"

He nods, and looks up at me.

"My dog is under there," I say, pointing underneath the barn, "and she won't come out! What should I do?!" I ask.

"Yeah, I thought I saw her go under there," he replies, smiling. He bends down and sees the dog.

"Maybe ... do you have any treats? That may get her out," he suggests.

"Treats! Great idea!" I tell him. "Yes! They're in my car. Do you mind standing here while I just run right over there," I point to the other side of the barn, "My car is parked right there."

He nods and takes the leash from me.

I start running down the road and I turn back for a second. He looks so funny standing there holding onto the pink leash with Meg no where to be seen.

Intuitively, I call, "Meg, I'm going to have fun, bye!!! Bye Meg!!!" and she comes out, running after me! Relieved, I start laughing, and I manage to grab her leash and get a hold of the dog.

"Thank you!!!!!" I call back to him. "You saved the day!!!!!! I really appreciate it! Thanks, again!"

He waves back to me, grinning, and Meg and I make it back to the food bank.

At the car, I pour her water and she practically drinks the entire gallon in one swoop. I wipe off the dirt with towels I have in the car.

Another man is standing there who I usually see at the food bank and he starts talking to us. "Hi, your dog is soooo beautiful."

"Awww, thank you."

I take out her brush and start brushing Meg, collecting heaps of her fur in my hands. She stands perfectly still while I do this. "Spa treatment," I tell her, and she let's me do my thing.

"She really enjoys that," he says, watching us.

His old, banged up car is parked near mine and he introduces himself as Jack. He begins telling me about his dogs, his life, and the depression meds he has been on for past twenty years.

Meanwhile, the food bank people have started to arrive and they like to come over and remind me, that "I'm too early," and "I have to wait," and I tell them "no problem."

They're all giving me dirty looks, and I wonder if it's the new car.

Mine is the nicest in the lot.

I put Meg in the car so she can rest, and I sit in the car with her while we wait in the heat for Angie's food.

One by one, people running the food bank come out to talk to me as I wait in the car. "You know, if you need to come early, I suggest that when you call in, you ask to be the first in line."

"No problem," I reply, "I don't need to be first, thanks."

Another woman comes out, "Can I see the dog?" she asks, bending over and breathing on me.

I'm trapped and can't move because I'm sitting in the car and she too, reminds me, "You're too early. There's a line."

There is no line, I know I am early, and let's just get it going.

"Thank you so much for your service!" I reply.

I debate whether or not to close my car window to avoid these conversations, but it's too hot for Meg.

My phone rings and it's Ricko.

"What are you doing?" he asks.

"Dog things, what's up?"

"I just found a great apartment for you here in LA. A friend of mine says it'll be avail…"

LA, I think.

When life was so good. And easy. With perfect weather. All the time.

I stop him. "I can't, Rick…"

I think of my aunt in the convent and how I am the only one who ever goes to visit her, and Angie, who depends on me for this food every week…And then there's my father…

"Rick, thanks, but I can't move now."

"What do you mean?"

"I have obligations…"

He's taken aback. "Obligations? You?"

"Rick, I'd love to, really," I say, "but I just can't…"

Somebody comes out of the food bank with my cart of food, and I tell Rick I have to go.

I put it all the groceries in the trunk of my car, careful not to crush the eggs for Angie, and I drive out, waving goodbye to Jack, the guy jacked up on his depression meds, and head over to Angie's.

It takes forty minutes to get over there because the roads along the Connecticut shoreline are only one lane and windy, but it's a scenic back road and beautiful drive.

I keep the windows open for Meg and she loves standing up on the passenger seat, and hanging her head out the window.

Once I'm at Angie's, I unload all the groceries into her kitchen, and ask her if she has any trash that needs to be taken out.

Once done, we are off again to the jewelry store.

I pull into the jewelry store, pay for my fixed necklace, and when I get home, I wash the necklace with soap and hot water, and I put it around my neck.

I look in the mirror.

I smile at myself.

My diamond is back on.

And *I'm sparkling again.*

Fifty-Two

Chapter 52

The call comes and the funeral is Friday. One of my father's cousin has died and, "Be there at the church for the mass at 11:00 a.m.," he tells me.

"Okay, Dad."

I was actually the one to break the news to him.

Ninety-five year old Angie was best friends with his mother who was 106 years old. They grew up together and Angie was calling me every day with his deteriorating condition.

I didn't think much of it at the time because all of her friends were in this "deteriorating condition," but by the end of the month, Angie called in a panic telling me that the maid told her that he died, but not to tell anybody.

Of course I texted my father and my aunt and uncle, who really are the last standing relatives on our side.

My aunt and uncle are on the next flight *conveniently to Florida*, so it's up to my father to go and represent, "The family."

I arrive early, and park in the lot.

I had run Meg earlier in the morning and I'm hoping that she'll be content to sit in the car.

I had to dig through my closet to find something to wear, and I realize I didn't have any clothes that were black or even black coats, and it's now October and there's a nip in the air.

When I asked my mother to "bring me something black," she ignored me, which didn't come as a surprise.

As I wait in the car for them to arrive, I adjust my long black suede boots that I haven't put on in years. I'm wearing a black suede skirt which is on the short side, and over it, I have on a dark green cashmere sweater that I had bought for the holidays that has gold buttons and white trim. Around my neck, I'm wear pearls, and I have on white gloves.

Because it's cold.

Over that, I'm wearing a beautiful white coat. "I just moved here from LA," I want to remind everybody, "Where nobody wears black."

The line of cars start pouring in, and I sit back in my seat and watch. Black Mercedes sedan after black Mercedes pulls in, and as I await my parents, they come rolling in, looking swank, and the car is clean and immaculate.

My father pulls up beside me, and nods. It's a nod that says, "Good thing you're here early."

I nod back, trying not to smile, because we're at a funeral and I know the vibe will be forlorn.

The man who died was eighty years old; he's younger than my father, and very well known in the community here and Palm Beach, Florida. He had his hands in all kinds of businesses and he's been arrested a few times, but that's all hush, hush in the family.

So the crowd is, how do I say… very well to do.

Class. A quiet class. *Quiet money.*

All of it.

When I was a young girl, my mother would pawn me off on Saturdays with my dad and every week I'd go with him to "the plant," the big block company that he owned. It was a family business; a cement company and it supplied the largest jobs in Ct and Manhattan.

Our routine on Saturdays was always the same; he'd put gas in the car while we were at the plant, drive around and watch things with me in the passenger seat, and then we'd go over to the car wash where he'd get his big Cadillac detailed.

My uncle owned it and he had a German Shepherd. The German Shepherd was named Shep.

And seeing this dog was the highlight of my week.

My uncle let the dog run free around the car wash and I'd follow it around, vying for its attention.

After that, my father took me to a private place in downtown New Haven. It looked like an abandoned building; it was a one story cement structure that had with no windows and no sign outside the door.

Expensive cars were always parked there in the lot. When you walked inside, it was a loud, underground establishment, packed with people, all men. The decor was expensive; lots of gold and deep burgundy colors with framed photos of our families that lined the wall.

My father would always say, "Don't tell your mother we came here."

I'd nod.

Not having any idea what "here," was.

Inside, my grandfather would sit at the end of the table with

261

my father beside him and my Uncle Fred would also be there sometimes. The men were all so regal and handsome with rosy cheeks, and they'd drink and sit back in their chairs, and talk and laugh. Sometimes it was serious.

My father would order me a Shirley Temple and I would just sit there and watch.

I never knew what to make of it, but this served me well when I went to work on Wall Street. Always the only woman, sitting at big tables with important men. I had clients, so many clients, and I served them well but most of what I knew and saw, I always kept to myself.

Until I needed to strike.

Which didn't happen often. Luckily.

Back at the funeral, my father parks in back of me, and he gets out of his Mercedes. I get out of my car to hug him.

He's in a business suit and still looks as young and as dapper and handsome as those old days.

I see my mother in the passenger seat, and I bend down to wave. She looks pretty; full makeup on and she's wearing black.

We all walk into the church together and sit in the few first front rows with the rest of the family.

The sons give a beautiful eulogy, and I can't help but dread the day that comes when I have to do this for my own parents, despite everything.

Afterwards, there's a reception at the yacht club and when we exit the church, my dad asks me if I know how to get there.

"Yes, you can follow me," I reply.

We all drive out of the church with the other cars, and down the windy roads of Connecticut towards the water. I have driven these roads a thousand times taking food to Angie and

Meg to the dog park. I feel confident, as if my days here are paying off.

It's a beautiful autumn day and the leaves on the trees are a colorful medley of oranges, yellows and reds.

We park next to each other at the yacht club, and I want to let Meg go to the bathroom, so my parents go in first.

I walk around the premises with Meg, and the water is sparkling beneath the warm sun. It's a beautiful day.

I put the dog back in the car, and when I walk inside, it's loud and filled with people, most I do not know. I make my way over to the children who gave the eulogy, and I tell what a beautiful job they did. I'm seated later next to my father and my mother at the table, and we're next to the now widow, my father's cousin.

She looks wrecked, and after being married to the same man for sixty years, I can't even imagine what her life will feel like now being alone.

As I look around the room, I see all my cousins have wonderful big families, with many children and even grandchildren. I have nothing and no one and I feel alone.

I eat the delicious food which is stuffed scrod with green beans and mashed potatoes and sliced roast beef and I take a napkin out of my purse and put some of the meat on it and take it out to Meg in the car.

She devours the meat as I sit half haphazardly on a stone wall with her on the leash.

I look all around and I'm not sure I want to go back inside.

A part of me thinks, *go back inside the yacht club, make connections, return to work on Wall Street, get it ALL back again...*

But I look down at Meg, who's looking up at me with those big brown eyes. She knows the park is right up the street, and instead, I get back in the car and I take her there.

We inhale the fresh air and start running around on the green grass, and I feel free and elated.

More than I ever have.

Meg is chasing the ball, and I am running after her even though I'm wearing a skirt. I always keep sneakers in my car for these situations!

It's well worth it!

I have three balls going and it's fun and it's fulfilling and for a moment, just a quick moment, I feel like I am exactly where I am meant to be, with her, right here in Connecticut.

We go back to the yacht club and arrive just in time to say goodbye to my parents who are leaving.

They have a long drive back, and as they lean their heads over to say goodbye to Meg in the car, with the sun behind them, I say, "Hang on! Let me take a photo!"

I take out my phone and snap a picture of them smiling, all dressed up, with the magnificent sun and blue sky behind them.

It's a close up of them. *And it's beautiful.*

I don't know what comes over me, but I instantly text it to my sister, and I include my parents on the text.

My sister replies: "Ahhh u wore the tie always pleasing your wife!!"

I am surprised at the response.

It's a dig.

You will never be anybody's wife, it says to me.

Maybe I'm reading it wrong. But when I get home to my quiet little home, and it's just me and my dog…

I realize…

I wouldn't have done it any other way.

Fifty-Three

Chapter 53

M eg has been acting weird. We have been seeing a lot of wild animals in the neighborhood and on our walks, we'd run into bobcats, clans of wild turkeys, skunks, and most recently, coyotes.

There's also a police shooting range nearby, and I know she hears the gunshots and gets scared.

She doesn't want to leave the house, so I've started walking without her.

It's weird not having her by my side. I don't feel safe. I'm all alone, and living in such a rural area, it frightens me.

After a few days of this, I had to do something, so I take her balls out of the trunk, slip on a flimsy backpack, and say, "Come on, Meg, let's go to the park!"

She knows the big park is about a mile down the road and being that it's still the height of autumn, it's always fun to walk through the piles of dried leaves. I have to lure her with the ball, but it works.

As we make our way down to the park, I'm dressed in a warm jacket and leggings and a corduroy baseball cap that really keeps my head warm with a white Yale knit pom pom hat over it.

We start running and playing in this huge field, and it's one of my favorite fields in the area; the grass is always well-kept, and I never lose her balls because I can easily find them in the trimmed grass.

On our way out, a lone man is walking towards us with his small, white little foo foo dog. Meg doesn't like those little dogs and neither do I, and foo foo starts barking.

Meg doesn't react or play with other dogs when she's with me; she rises above it, as if she's saying, *"Sorry, I'm playing with my mom right now, bye."*

But today, she runs up to the little barking dog.

The man is holding his dog on its leash in this big park, and he looks up at me in horror.

I smile and say, "Oh, don't worry, she's friendly. Is yours?"

He doesn't respond.

He's a middle aged man, dressed in preppy clothes and he looks like a snob. When Meg approaches his dog, she takes her long legs and knocks the dog down.

The little dog is now on its back, kicking its legs up in the air, whimpering, and if it could speak, it's saying, *"Stop! Help! Please!!"*

I can't help but giggle but the man doesn't find it funny at all, and he turns to me with a look on his face that says, GET YOUR DOG TO STOP! NOW!!

I take the ball in my hand and throw it the opposite direction of Foo Foo while ordering Meg to, "GET THE BALL!!!"

Meg takes off after it, and situation mitigated. "Sorry about that," I say, and we continue our way out of the park.

The real problem arises when we arrive to the main road, and Meg stops and won't move.

I turn back to her, "Let's go, Meg, time to go home."

But she WON'T BUDGE.

I pull on her leash, and NOTHING. Try, as you might, to lug a seventy pound plus beast to go in your direction when they don't want to, and it's hopeless. They are strong. And stubborn.

She must smell the animals, I think. *Or maybe she hears the gunshots.* I stand there as traffic is breezing by and I don't know what to do. I hate this main road, the cars go way too fast, but it's the only road to take us to the park and back.

I see the guy with the foo foo dog, the only other person in the park, has a pick up truck.

Maybe he'll give us a ride...

I NEED HELP. I walk around with Meg to find him.

He's now on the other side, still holding his little prissy poodle snickerdoodle, or whatever those dogs are called. When he sees me coming toward him with Meg, he looks alarmed again.

"Ohhhh, hiiiiiiiiiii," I say, much friendlier this time.

"Yes? Yes?" he asks, nervously, while grabbing foo foo in his hands.

I try not to laugh, and I try to establish a rapport. "How's it going?!" I ask, all friendly. Not working, he doesn't reply.

"Ummmm, I was wondering," I begin, "You see me and the dog seemed to be trapped. For whatever reason she's having trouble walking on the main road."

"So?! So?!" he repeats.

I'm not getting anywhere.

"Well, do you know if by any chance, there's any back trails we can take through the woods?"

I know there's not, I would never walk through the woods given all the wild life in the area, but I think it's a good conversation starter.

But it's not.

Out of his mouth comes more terror like comments, "No! No! I don't know anything, I don't know anything ABOUT THAT!"

"I see," I reply, remaining calm, thinking to myself this guy is never going to help me.

But he must.

I follow him around with Meg through the park.

We're walking beside him, and it's awkward and he seems peeved, "You know, I just don't know what's wrong with my dog... She seems to be afraid of something..."

"She's not afraid!" he sneers back, "she looks fine, we have to go, bye," and he jangles his car keys as if he's ready to escape me as we stand back in the parking lot.

Not so fast, buster.

You're not going *ANYWHERE WITHOUT ME.*

"Look," I state, very seriously, "WE NEED HELP!"

He doesn't respond.

I speak louder, "We're going to have to call the police!"

Like how I did that? It's now a "we," situation.

"What are the police going to do?!" he stammers.

"My dog WON'T MOVE and I NEED HELP, and somebody needs to come HELP ME!"

"I.... I don't know what the police are going to do."

"They're GOING TO DRIVE US HOME! THAT'S WHAT

THEY'RE GOING TO DO!"

I notice Meg now looking up at me with eyes that say, *Oh, no, Mom is coming unwound. Look out.*

I finally just come out and say it, "Look can you please just throw us in the back of your truck and drive us down the road? I only live a few blocks away."

"No, no! I can't."

I stand there stunned.

"How about you just go get your own car and I'll wait here with your dog," he comes back with.

I would never leave Meg alone with this guy, and not only that, it will take me at least an hour to walk all the way home and then come back with the car.

"Come on, please help me."

I look at him with pleading eyes, even though I'm wearing sunglasses.

He relents. He unlatches the back of his truck and I jump in before he can change his mind.

He looks down at Meg and says, "The dog will never make the jump."

"Oh, yes she will!"

I look down at her, and start to giggle. "Come on, Meggie, come on! JUMP!"

She's looking up at me confused.

"Grab her leash!" I tell the guy, "and hand it to me!"

He's more well behaved than the dog. He picks up the leash on the ground and hands it to me.

"Jump, Meg! COME ON!!"

And in one swoosh, on her hind legs Meg flies up into the pickup truck with me. The guy shakes his head, as if he is stunned, and asks where I live. I tell him to just start driving and I'm only right down the road, and I'll tell him where to stop through the back window.

He starts driving, and I grab a hold of the side of the truck, with my other hand on Meg, and he starts going fast, and it's fun and I start laughing.

I'm having a ball and it reminds me of when I once left an Italian nightclub, and I got on the back of a motorcycle with some hottie in the middle of the night and we sped around Italy.

I hold onto Meg, and we get caught in a traffic jam.

School has just been let out and so we're surrounded by school buses, and all the children are looking out the window and pointing at us and laughing, and I start waving as if I'm the Queen of England on the back of a chariot.

I start waving my hand around in the air, giddy. "Hiiiiii!!!"

The guy keeps looking at me as he drives trying to figure out where to dump me and when we arrive to our street, he stops and let's us out.

"OH, THANK YOU SO MUCH!!! THANK YOU THANK YOU!!!!" I say, over and over again, genuinely grateful.

He barely says anything at all to us, and as I turn to watch him go, his truck gets jammed up on the curve in the grass when he tries to do a U turn, but he manages to maneuver it out.

I'm pleased and another stressful situation is diverted.

The next week, Meg stops walking with me altogether.

She doesn't fall for the backpack and ball trick and she refuses to leave our front yard, so I have to put her in the car and drive her to the park.

I had been writing all morning and I had what's known as "book brain," and I don't really like to drive with that, but I take her to the park anyway to blow off steam.

We run and do our thing, and I can keep my eye on my Mercedes in the lot, and as I do, I I see the black truck there again.

I wonder if it's that same guy, but all I see in the distance is two young looking men walking on the other side of the park.

Meg and I keep playing with her ball, and when they come closer to us, I realize it IS THE MAN with his son.

They are walking are the park in a slow, confused manner staring down at the ground. They seem to be in a very downcast mood (surprise, surprise) and I wave. "Hi!!! You're the guy who gave me the ride home that day, right?!"

This time, he doesn't have his foo foo dog.

"Yes, yes," he dismisses me, "It's me, but I'm sorry, I can't give you a ride today because I don't have my key."

Wow.

He's blowing me off already. What a jerk off. I didn't even ask him for a ride!

"Don't worry," I reply with a large grin, "I drove my car today, so you're off the HOOK!" and I laugh.

He doesn't find it funny, shrugs me off, and I just keep walking with Meg.

When we pass them again, I say, "Hey, have you guys been seeing all the wild animals around here?! I saw a coyote the other day, and I'm worried…"

He cuts me off. "We haven't seen anything. I lost the key, and we're looking for it."

What did he say?

I know I have book brain, but did he just say he lost his key?

"Wait," I ask, "You mean, you lost your car key here – in the park?!"

"Yes! Yes! That's what I told you!"

"OOOOOhhhhh!!!!" I see. "Oh, that's terrible! Well, I'm really good at finding things," I tell him. "I'll help you!"

He huffs me off, AGAIN and keeps walking.

I can't help to think what an asshole this guy is, but he helped me out that day. *And damnit I need to help him find his keys.*

I look up across the vast park, and suddenly I realize, there's no way I can find his keys. This park is way too big and I'll be here all day. I've already been here an hour with Meg, my arthritis is starting to hurt, and I need to get back home and rest.

But I can't abandon him.

Not in his time of need. He helped me after all.

Think smart. Think!!!!

"Meg, find it!" I command. She has been learning that trick at home, but she needs to smell the item first, but I hope maybe she can pick up his scent. We were in the back of his truck.

But maybe not.

I look up and I look at where the guy's truck is parked. I remembered that when I first saw them earlier, they were walking on the very far side of the park, so I start walking more in the center.

I say a pray to St. Anthony who is the saint to help you find things.

I rarely take advantage of this unless *I really need to find something* and I *really want to help this guy.*

"Just take me to the keys, God," I whisper under my breath, and literally in less than ninety seconds, I am led to his keys.

I find them there on the ground in front of me.

"I FOUND IT!!!!!!!" I SCREAM.

I look up for them, and they are not even close. They are

diagonally opposite from me in the park. "I FOUND IT!!!!!!!"
I SCREAM AGAIN. I take the chuck it stick that's in my hand
and I start waving it like an SOS. "I FOUND THE KEYS!!!!!!"

They look up and hear me, and start running towards me.

I don't want to pick up their keys because my hands are
filled with Meg's saliva from playing with her balls.

The son gets there first, and I point to them lying in the
ground.

"Oh, thank you!" he says, and picks them up. "This is great!"
He waves the keys in the direction of his father. "Wow, we
didn't think we'd find them!"

"No problem," I say, "Glad I could help," and I take off to get
Meg some water in the car.

As I'm rummaging through the back of my trunk cleaning
Meg's balls, they are driving out of the parking lot.

The guy pulls over beside me and rolls down his window. I
turn and I start giggling, anxious to see what he's going to say
to me.

"KARMA!!!!!" he says, laughing. "KARMA!!!!!!!!!!"

I laugh back with him. "Good deed for good deed!!!!!"

His son passes me next and he rolls down his window. "You
saved our Wednesday, thank you."

I grin, and I'm floored.

What a day, I think.

What a pay back.

I'm still grinning and feel so grateful for this experience. For
this restoration in humanity that having Meg has given me.

I will always remember all those people who have helped
me along the way...From my neighbors in that first apartment
complex in South Carolina, to Pixie and her trio of dogs, to
all those nice people at the hotels who took us in, and all the

people who just stop to tell me how cute Meg is…

Every second, where I get to see beauty and love and grace through owning this precious animal is a priceless, wonderful gift.

And I wouldn't trade it for anything.

Fifty-Four

Chapter 54

It's a random Thursday, and I get a text from my mother: Saturdy, lobster place on the water, we cn meet u 4 lunch.
I read it and I'm surprised because

1. She never wants to be with me. 2. Her English now appears to be so broken, I am wondering if she's losing her mind.

She was the one who taught me how to read, write, and more importantly, grammer, and she was a stickler with all of that. She was that woman with the "dictionary," on the table by her couch so she could look up the words that she did not know or could not spell. This was one of the many things I loved about my mother and admired.

"Sure!" I write back, "Sounds great, Mom, thank you."

I get a series of her "emoji's," back from her. One is in the shape of a giraffe, our favorite animal.

That Saturday, I get to the lobster restaurant early, and this place has the best lobster rolls in all of Connecticut.

I park my car in the empty lot, and go inside. I find the manager and tell him I will be paying for lunch. I have done this before when we met here and it's a cash only place so it's an easy transaction.

He nods and smiles.

After that, Meg and I cross the road and hit the beach. It's a beautiful Indian summer day... late October and the weather is warm.

The water is calm and Meg runs in the waves.

I'm having a hard time running with her because I am wearing these overly big new Ray Ban sunglasses that are supposed to be for my new eye prescription.

I had seen my old childhood eye doctor and he gave me a great new prescription, but the guy at the lenses shop can't seem to get my order right.

He ordered the wrong size frames and lenses and I had to wait weeks for new ones to arrive, numerous times.

Meg gets to run for a good hour before my parents arrive, and when they do, my mother looks beautiful as usual. For her age, she really brings it, same with my father who always is wearing new clothes, and when my father goes inside to get our food, I am sitting outside with my mother and Meg.

Meg, is exhausted underneath the table, and I say, nonchalantly, "Mom, too bad Auntie Phil couldn't come. I was happy to pick her up and bring her."

Auntie Phil is her sister who lives in the next town over who she hasn't seen in months but she starts to come unwound and asks, "What are you, trying to start trouble, Julie?!"

"Mom?" I ask, my jaw dropping, "What do you mean?"

"Do NOT START ANY TROUBLE TODAY. YOUR FA-

THER HAD A LONG DRIVE AND HE IS TIRED. TIRED. TIRED!!!! At our age, we CANNOT do it ANYMORE!!!"

My heart sinks and I'm at a loss for words.

My father comes out of the restaurant with the food, it is 11:00 in the morning and there's no one around us, and who wants butter drenched lobster and fried clam strips at this hour, but I dig in and try to make small talk.

I decide its best not to ask about their health, so I talk about my glasses situation.

"These glasses," I announce, as I try to push them higher up on my nose because they keep falling down, "are the wrong size. The people at the glasses shop just couldn't get it right. I had SPECIFICALLY MARKED on each glasses case, this one is for the distance lenses, and this frame is for the reading lenses...."

Chomp, chomp, they're chewing their food, and hardly listening to me.

"And what happens? I go walk Meg for two hours to wait for the installation because that's how long it takes, and I come back and they give me the glasses, they COMPLETELY SCREW it up putting the wrong lenses into the wrong frames! So I had to WAIT two MORE weeks for them to order the NEW lenses since these SPECIAL LENSES come from Japan, and what happens next when those finally come — they put the left lense into the right eye and the other... screwing it UP AGAIN."

They get the picture and nod.

Now here's where my mother usually comes in and says something like: "You're just not speaking clearly. You are not explaining it right. You probably wrote down the wrong instructions. You gave them the wrong prescription. YOU.

DID. IT. WRONG. *AND IT IS YOUR FAULT.*

But what comes out of my mother's mouth is not that at all. "You have to be your own advocate, Juliana. Nobody cares."

She puts another fried clam into her mouth, and repeats, "Nobody cares."

I'm stunned. "Exactly, mom! I agree! That's what I always say!"

My dad doesn't say anything and just keeps eating.

"I mean, CAN YOU BELIEVE IT!?" I ask her again. "The stupidity!"

"Of course I can," my mother replies, calmly. "It's the world we're living in today. Nobody cares. Nobody gives A SHIT. And they get away with it."

I laugh.

I'm so surprised. *Wow.*

Just wow.

For the first time I think in my life, my mother agrees with me and she's on my side.

My demeanor from this point on changes.

I feel restored. *Validated.*

Heard.

Later, after lunch, we all walk on the beach together, and it's a glorious day. Meg takes off for the water again, and I kick off my shoes and run after her.

We're splashing in the waves and having a grand ol' time.

My mother and father are seated back on the boardwalk on a bench, and I wave to them from the water.

My mom is staring into her phone.

I turn back to Meg, and we keep splashing and running in the calm waters of the Long Island Sound, and the sun is hot and it feels good. The heat helps with my arthritis, and the dog, well, she helps *with everything.*

For an instant, this moment reminds me of an ending to a long Hollywood movie, where the characters are finally happy, and they have endured, and all is well in the world. And camera rises above, as the music plays and the credits roll.

It's a bitter sweet moment, and one I waited a long time for. Peace and serenity and even a tad of security at last.

And this is you. This is me.

This is *all of us.*

Fifty-Five

Chapter 55

~~~∞⚬∞~~~

The next morning, I wake up and enter the living room to see my love bug, Meg.

She's sleeping peacefully on the twin bed, and I cover her up to keep her warm with my Ralph Lauren warm flannel shirt.

She looks as snug as a bug.

"My little love girl…. Did you sleep good?!" I bend down to kiss her head.

She rolls over so I can rub her belly, and I love her; in a thousand million different ways, I love her.

I get ready to sit down at my desk and write.

I'm coming up toward the end of this book and I look out my open window, hear the birds, and the fresh breeze hits my cheeks.

I feel a sense of peace and gratitude for the basic necessities of life. And though life sometimes feel paused, I look at my lovely landscaped yard, listening to the wind chimes that my neighbors have hanging from their trees, and it's a simple life here in Connecticut that the dog and I have created.

I find great joy in relaxing on my rocker on my porch, I love cooking my meals from scratch, and baking my own desserts.

I love the walks we take in the neighborhood, and the changing of the seasons.

I was hoping that by the end of this book, something climatic would have happened; Hollywood calls and my movie is getting made, or Noel calls, or my sister calls with an apology, or I make tons of money that I lost in the stock market, back.

But none of that has happened.

But I know the mystery of what's going to happen next is absolutely extraordinary.

And if I just stay positive, everything will work out above and beyond anything than I could have ever figured out...

I stare at the blank screen, and for whatever reason, I decide to call my sister. My mother said she was having a host of eye problems, so I want to see how she's feeling.

"Hi," I say, when she picks up.

"Oh, Julie, hi." She still sounds like she's ten years old to me.

"How's it going? How are your eyes?" I ask.

"Good," she replies.

She's just like my father. Never much to say... or divulge... or complain about for that matter.

She just takes it all in stride. "How about you?" she asks.

"I'm waiting for this guy to bring me my new set of glasses," I tell her. "I am so frustrated, he has has made a thousand mistakes. It's a miracle I haven't blown a gasket by now..."

I hear the "Umm hmmm," snicker in her voice.

Just more Julie drama, I imagine her thinking.

"Anyhow, some good news on Mom! When I was telling her about all the problems I was going through with my glasses over the weekend while we were having lobster here in Connecticut…"

I pause to see if she's even listening.

"Yeah?" she asks.

"Welp, she agreed with me, Sarah! She actually sided with me! Can you believe it?! Instead of blaming me like she always does, she said, 'You have to be your own advocate! Nobody cares! Nobody!' Can you believe it?!"

"I guess so," she sighs, "but did you ever ask yourself why at your age, I mean you're in your fifties, do you need your mother's approval anyhow?"

I catch my breath. Her words cut to my core. And she knows it.

"I don't need mommy's approval. It was just different, Sarah, she *agreed with me*. She sided with me. *For once*. And you know what, I felt heard."

"Hmmmfff," she replies.

"HmmmFFFFF," I sneer back. I glance out the window, and see the guy arriving with my new glasses.

Meg starts barking and he just leaves them at the front door as instructed.

"Anyhow, I don't know if you remember this story I told you before, but when I was living in LA and listening to one of the greatest TV writers of all time tell a story about the theme of his writing, which is insanely successful," I add for effect, "He told the group this great story about his mother and his words always stuck with me."

"What did he say?"

"He said, 'The day finally came when I realized that like a

construction worker who has a toolbox with nails, hammers, chainsaws, etc., so he can build, he needs those tools in his toolbox to be a construction worker. But my mother,' he said, 'in her toolbox, she didn't have the tools to be a mother. Her toolbox was empty. And I no longer resented her for that. Because how can you resent someone for not giving you something that they don't have.'"

Dead silence.

"So I've accepted it, Sarah, a long time ago. I have risen up."

But did I really?

Is my sister right? Am I constantly seeking my mother's validation?

More silence on her end and MEDICARE is calling and I need to enroll, and I have been waiting for this phone call forever, and tell her I have to go.

Two long hellacious hours later on the phone with Medicare, our country's world class healthcare system *(cough, cough,)* I hang up and I'm drained.

I realize it now has been two years since I've been on disability and since I have had Meg.

I turn to look out the window again, and the leaves are all but fallen from the trees. It's almost December and winter is upon us.

I realize I am not going to Florida this winter. There's still is no housing or stock market crash, and it's going to just be more of the same. And I accept it.

I get up to open the front door, and I reach for my new glasses.

I bring them inside, wash them with soap and water, and then I put them on my face.

They're perfect.

When I sit back down at my desk, my cell phone dings.

I look at it.

It's a text from my mother.

There are no words. It's just a video.

I click on the video, and it starts to play...

And what I see astonishes me.

It's a video of me Meg and I ... From the weekend...

We're playing in the water on the beach...laughing, and running in the waves, chasing each other.

It instantly reminds me of that video my mother would play over and over again of her and my sister, dancing and laughing with each other on the beach, with that Natalie Merchant song playing in the background....*These Are The Days*.

I cannot believe it.

I watch the video again and again.

I look so happy.

We look so happy.

And I'm amazed.

I am amazed that she captured it. While I thought my mother was staring at her phone ignoring me, she was actually filming us.

As Meg and I run up and down the beach, the sun is in back of us hitting us in a glorious light.

I pull up the song "These Are The Days," and I listen to it on my computer.

It's a song about growing and blooming, and suddenly I remember the quote from the convent from Mother Clelia when I spent those precious weeks there with my aunt.

"At the end of the sorrowful journey,

You will be permitted to look backward;

then you will see with joyful astonishment,

The furrow you dug with such pain,
All blossoming behind you."
— Mother Clelia Merloni
And as the Natalie Merchant song plays, I realize I no longer hate the song.

Maybe I never did.

So I'll end the story with the great quote from GORDON GEKKO, of the movie, WALL STREET...

"If you need a friend, get a dog.

It's trench warfare out there, pal." — Gordon Gekko

LOL.

Peace out. XO

* * *

About the Author

Juliana Jones started her career at Robertson Stephens working in the Venture Capital Distribution group, was promoted to Institutional Sales, and then transferred to New York where she was hired at Morgan Stanley as a Senior Vice President. She ended her career at Carlin Financial, the firm talked about in Michael Lewis' financial thriller Flash Boys.

Currently, she is Chief Investment Strategist, Proprietary Trading Account, Citygirl Holdings. ❤ Volatility trader. 💰 She day trades and then taste lattes ☕ around the world.

(I guess I need to rewrite this... LOL)

Be sure to check out all the Meg photos here!! ❤❤★★★★★
  https://www.citygirllovescoffee.com/megsphotos

We love our fans !!! 👄👄

CONTACT:

Media inquiries/Book signings: julianajonesHEDGED@gmail.com
  Website: www.citygirllovescoffee.com

SOCIAL:

Twitter: @citygirlj
  Instagram: @citygirljuliana
  Stocktwits: @citygirlj
  Facebook: @citygirlj7
  Website: www.citygirllovescoffee.com

HEDGED by JULIANA JONES
Read how it all began...

When Jolette Marco blows up her account in a day trade gone awry, she dives into a morally corrupt abyss of Wall Street to earn it all back, and finds danger with a hedge fund gang member who steals her heart, giving new meaning to the words, "I lost everything."

THE VALENTINE'S DAY CONCERT by JULIANA JONES
Does Jolette really stop trading? And is this the end of her and Noel? Find out here...!

She ropes a Hollywood playboy into going to the Barry Manilow concert in Las Vegas on Valentine's Day. What could possibly go wrong?